GOODBYE
A STORY OF SUICIDE

Written by **HAILEE JOY LAMBERTH**

Art by **DONALD HUDSON**

Inked by **JOSE MARZAN JR**

Colors by **MONICA KUBINA**

Lettering by **JIMMY BETANCOURT**
and **TYLER SMITH** ~~for Comi~~

Zuiker Press

Los Angeles

GOODBYE: A STORY OF SUICIDE

© 2020 Zuiker Press

Hailee Joy Lamberth Photographs © 2020 Jennifer Lamberth

Written by Anthony E. Zuiker
Illustrated by Donald Hudson
Cover pencils and inks by Donald Hudson
Colors by Monica Kubina
Cover colors by Monica Kubina
Ink by Jose Marzan Jr.
Lettering by Jimmy Betancourt and Tyler Smith for Comicraft
Designed by Roberta Melzl
Edited by Rob Tokar

Founders: Michelle & Anthony E. Zuiker
Publisher: David Wilk

Published by Zuiker Press
16255 Ventura Blvd.
Suite #900
Encino, CA 91436
United States of America

Visit us online at www.zuikerpress.com

ISBN 1-947378-27-8 (hardcover)
ISBN 978-1-947378-29-2 (ebook)

PRINTED IN CANADA
April 2020
10 9 8 7 6 5 4 3 2 1

DEDICATED TO ... every young person who needs to be reminded they are not alone.

HOPE lies within these pages.

ZUIKER PRESS

... is a husband and wife publishing company that champions the voices of young authors. We are an **ISSUE-BASED** literary house. All of our authors have elected to tell their personal stories and be ambassadors of their cause. Their goal, as is ours, is that young people will learn from their pain and heroics and find **HOPE**, **CHANGE**, and **HAPPINESS** in their own lives.

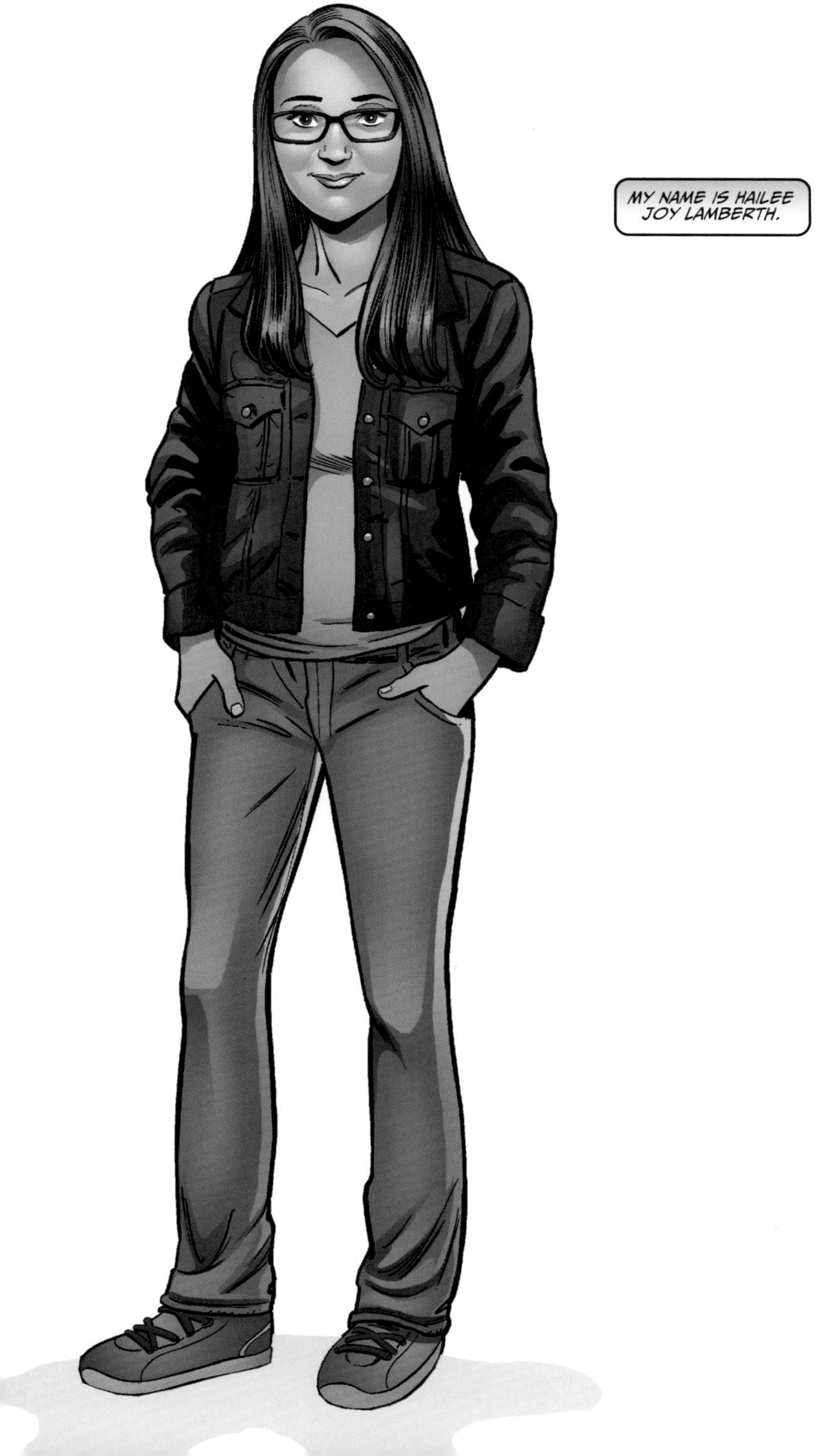
MY NAME IS HAILEE JOY LAMBERTH.

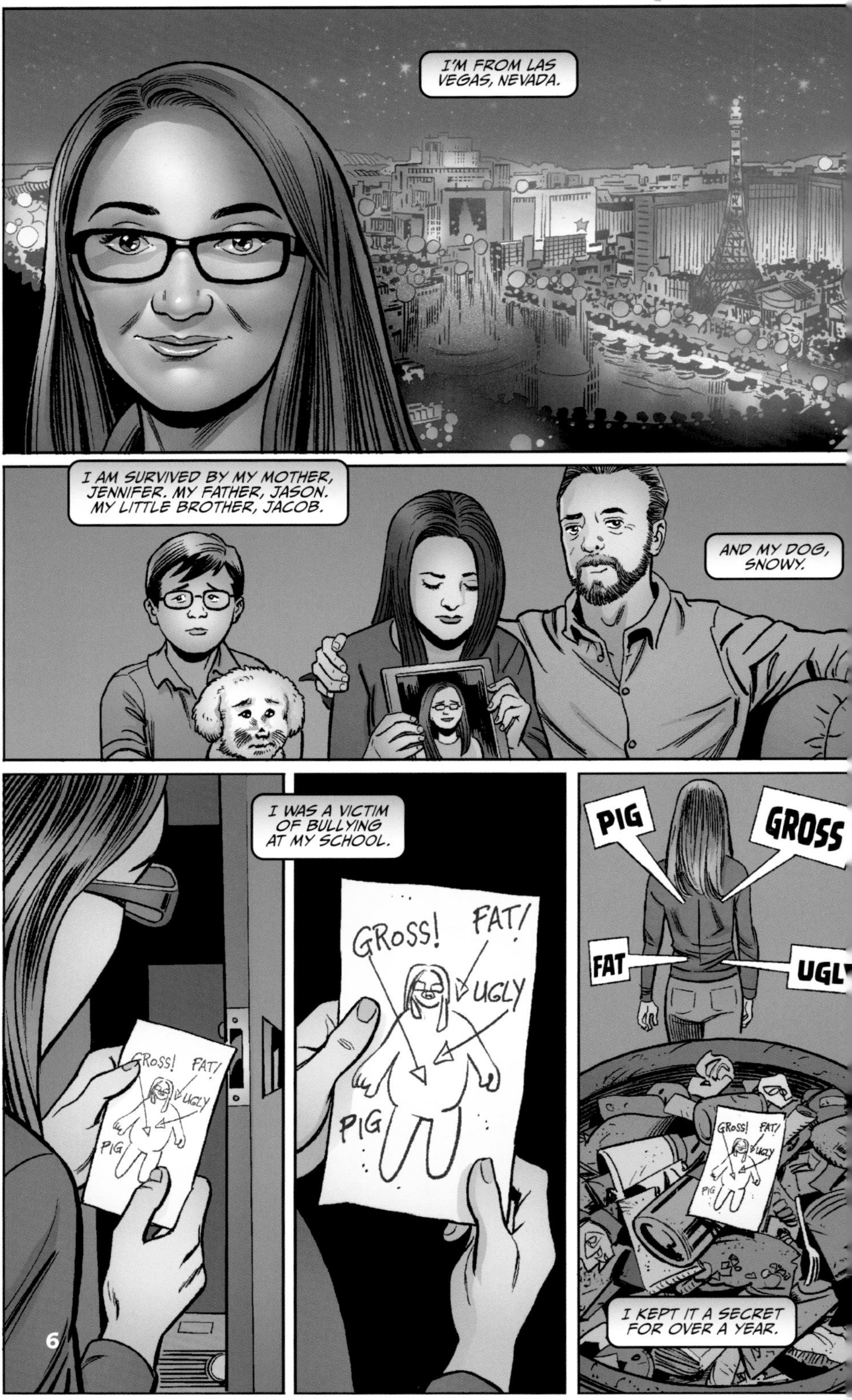

I'M FROM LAS VEGAS, NEVADA.
I AM SURVIVED BY MY MOTHER, JENNIFER. MY FATHER, JASON. MY LITTLE BROTHER, JACOB.
AND MY DOG, SNOWY.
GROSS! FAT!
UGLY
PIG
I WAS A VICTIM OF BULLYING AT MY SCHOOL.
GROSS! FAT!
UGLY
PIG
PIG
GROSS
FAT
UGL
I KEPT IT A SECRET FOR OVER A YEAR.

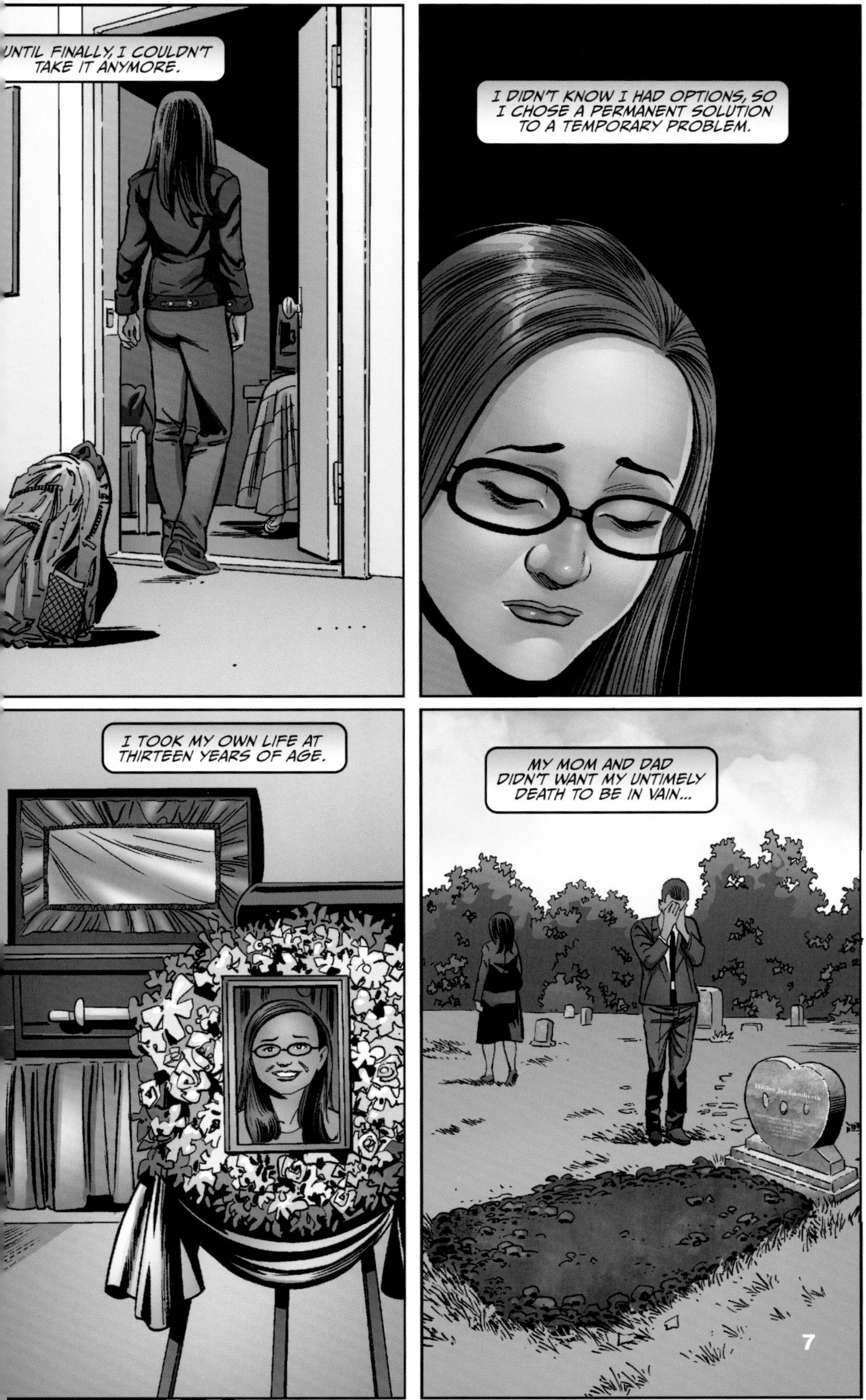
UNTIL FINALLY, I COULDN'T TAKE IT ANYMORE.
I DIDN'T KNOW I HAD OPTIONS, SO I CHOSE A PERMANENT SOLUTION TO A TEMPORARY PROBLEM.
I TOOK MY OWN LIFE AT THIRTEEN YEARS OF AGE.
MY MOM AND DAD DIDN'T WANT MY UNTIMELY DEATH TO BE IN VAIN...

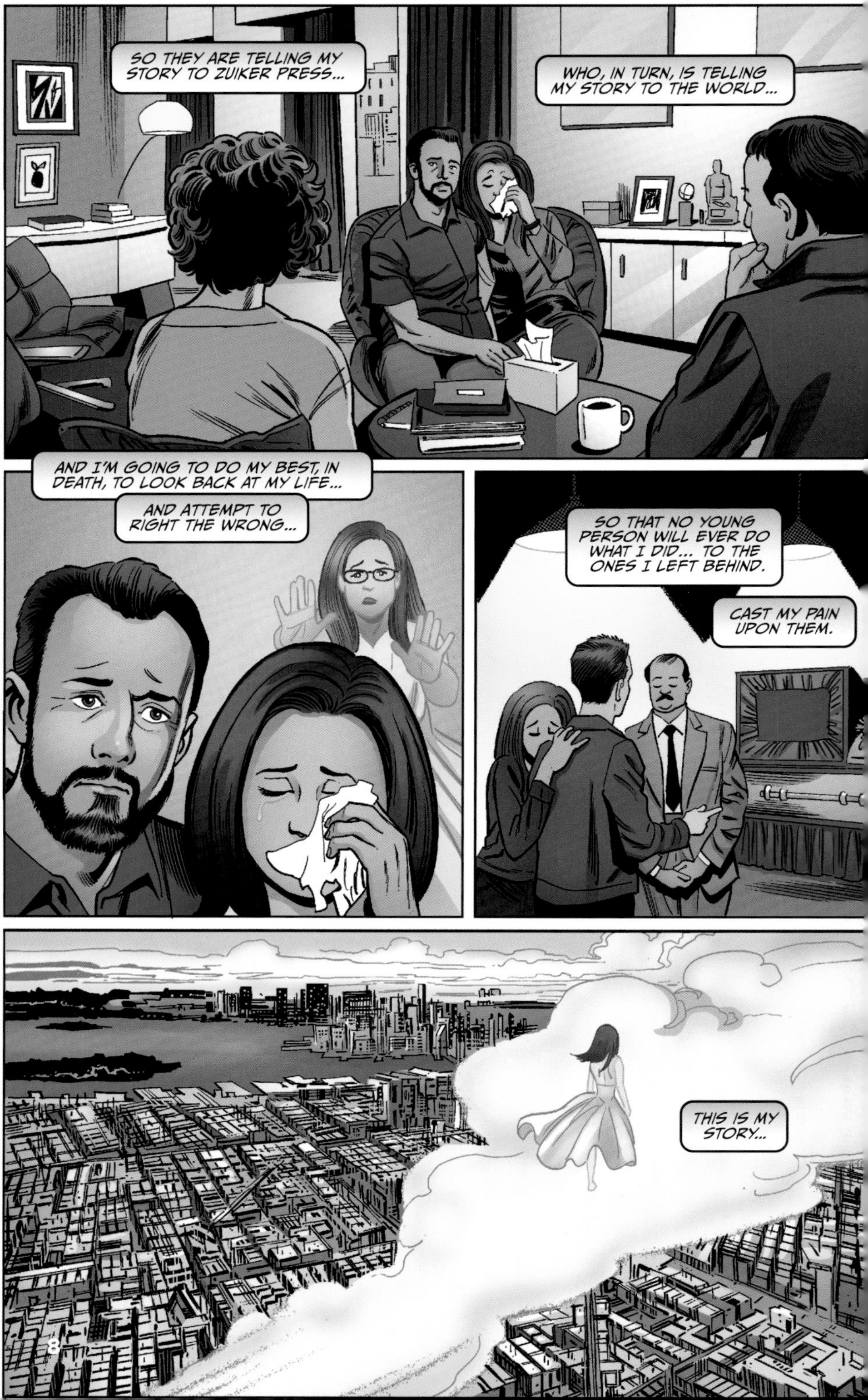
SO THEY ARE TELLING MY STORY TO ZUIKER PRESS...
WHO, IN TURN, IS TELLING MY STORY TO THE WORLD...
AND I'M GOING TO DO MY BEST, IN DEATH, TO LOOK BACK AT MY LIFE...
AND ATTEMPT TO RIGHT THE WRONG...
SO THAT NO YOUNG PERSON WILL EVER DO WHAT I DID... TO THE ONES I LEFT BEHIND.
CAST MY PAIN UPON THEM.
THIS IS MY STORY...

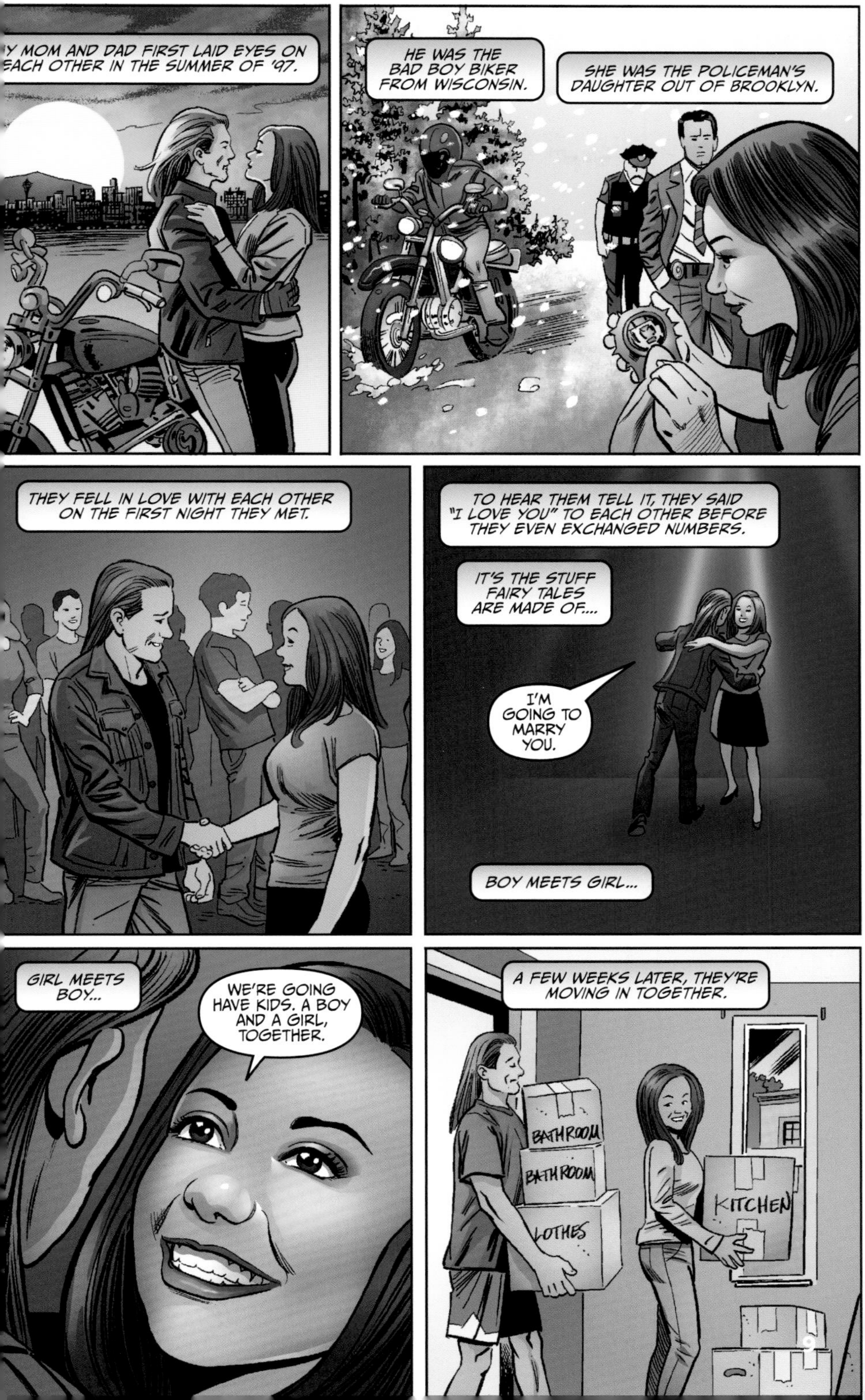
Y MOM AND DAD FIRST LAID EYES ON EACH OTHER IN THE SUMMER OF '97.
HE WAS THE BAD BOY BIKER FROM WISCONSIN.
SHE WAS THE POLICEMAN'S DAUGHTER OUT OF BROOKLYN.
THEY FELL IN LOVE WITH EACH OTHER ON THE FIRST NIGHT THEY MET.
TO HEAR THEM TELL IT, THEY SAID "I LOVE YOU" TO EACH OTHER BEFORE THEY EVEN EXCHANGED NUMBERS.
IT'S THE STUFF FAIRY TALES ARE MADE OF....
I'M GOING TO MARRY YOU.
BOY MEETS GIRL...
GIRL MEETS BOY...
WE'RE GOING HAVE KIDS. A BOY AND A GIRL, TOGETHER.
A FEW WEEKS LATER, THEY'RE MOVING IN TOGETHER.
BATHROOM
BATHROOM
LOTHES
KITCHEN

A FEW YEARS LATER, MY MOTHER'S GOT A PREGNANCY STICK IN HER HAND.

PRE... ...T...

MY FATHER LOOKED AT THAT STICK LIKE IT WAS AN ALGEBRA PROBLEM.

HE WENT TO THE STORE TO BUY EIGHT MORE STICKS.

3

AND SURE AS YOU CAN SAY, "DOUBLE LINE MEANS PREGGERS..."

THEY WERE HAVING A BABY. ME...

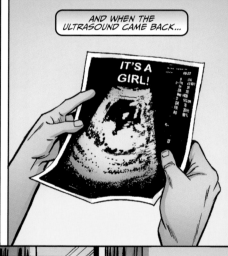

AND WHEN THE ULTRASOUND CAME BACK...

IT'S A GIRL!

NEXT THING YOU KNOW, MY FATHER TRADED HIS LONG HAIR AND MOTORCYCLE...

... FOR A HAIRCUT AND NURSERY BOOKS.

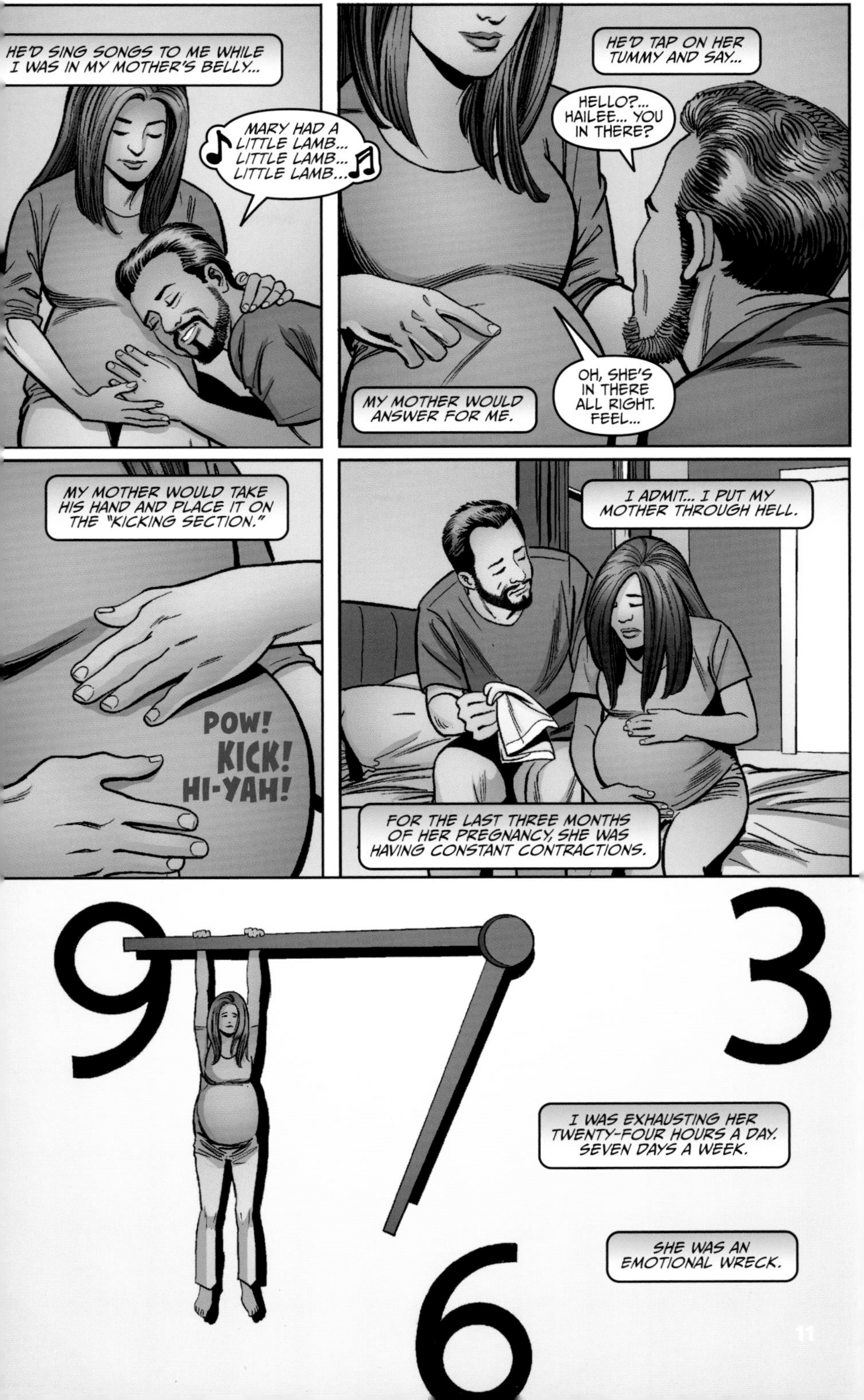
HE'D SING SONGS TO ME WHILE I WAS IN MY MOTHER'S BELLY...
MARY HAD A LITTLE LAMB... LITTLE LAMB... LITTLE LAMB...
HE'D TAP ON HER TUMMY AND SAY...
HELLO?... HAILEE... YOU IN THERE?
MY MOTHER WOULD ANSWER FOR ME.
OH, SHE'S IN THERE ALL RIGHT. FEEL...
MY MOTHER WOULD TAKE HIS HAND AND PLACE IT ON THE "KICKING SECTION."
POW!
KICK!
HI-YAH!
I ADMIT... I PUT MY MOTHER THROUGH HELL.
FOR THE LAST THREE MONTHS OF HER PREGNANCY, SHE WAS HAVING CONSTANT CONTRACTIONS.
9
3
6
I WAS EXHAUSTING HER TWENTY-FOUR HOURS A DAY. SEVEN DAYS A WEEK.
SHE WAS AN EMOTIONAL WRECK.

FINALLY, I WAS READY TO ARRIVE...

DECEMBER

	1	2	3	4	5	6
7	8	9	10	11	12	13
14	15	16	17	18	19	20
21	22	23	24	25	26	27
28	29	30	31			

I WAS BORN ON DECEMBER 10, 2000.

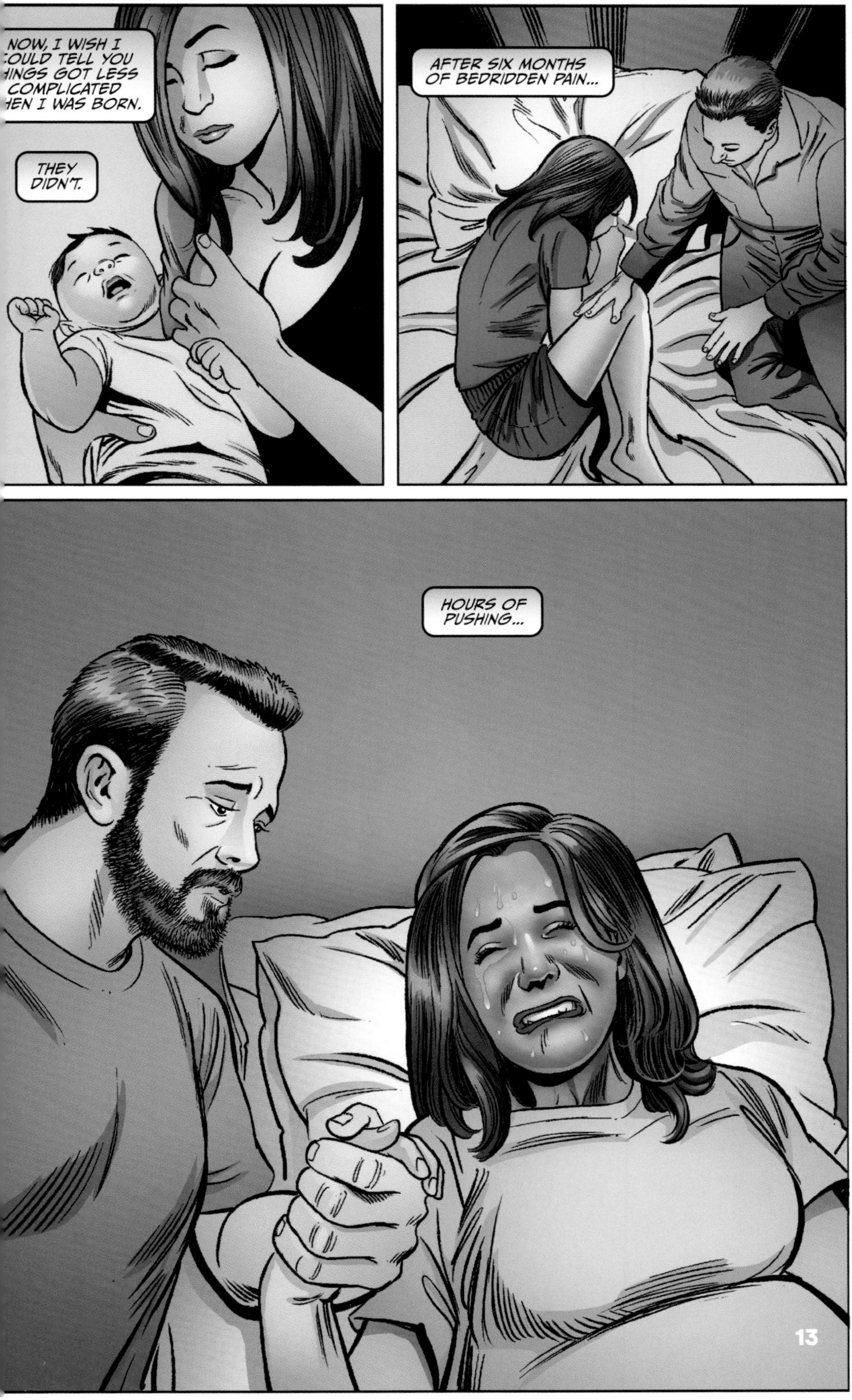
NOW, I WISH I COULD TELL YOU HINGS GOT LESS COMPLICATED HEN I WAS BORN.
THEY DIDN'T.
AFTER SIX MONTHS OF BEDRIDDEN PAIN...
HOURS OF PUSHING...

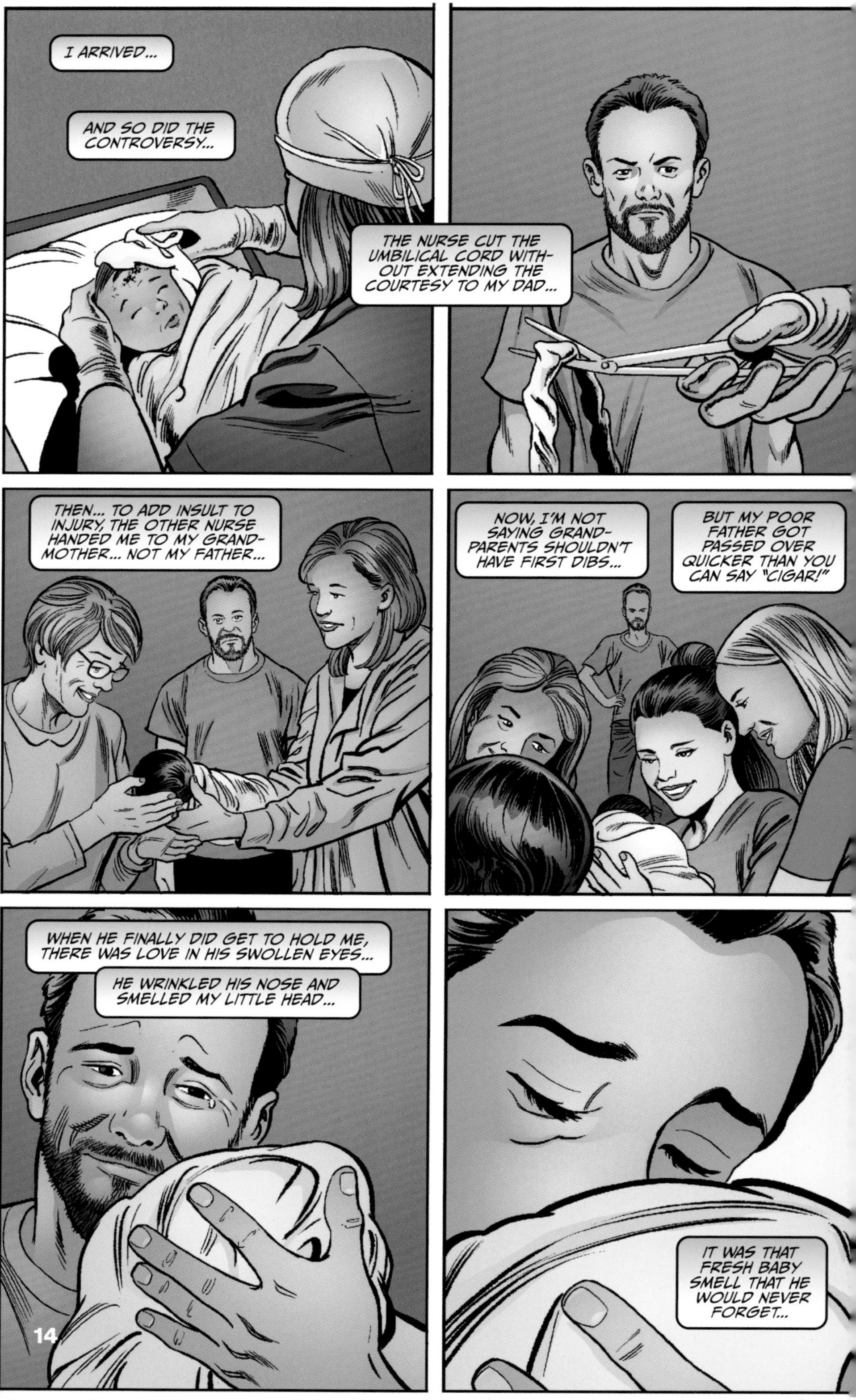
I ARRIVED...
AND SO DID THE CONTROVERSY...
THE NURSE CUT THE UMBILICAL CORD WITH-OUT EXTENDING THE COURTESY TO MY DAD...
THEN... TO ADD INSULT TO INJURY, THE OTHER NURSE HANDED ME TO MY GRAND-MOTHER... NOT MY FATHER...
NOW, I'M NOT SAYING GRAND-PARENTS SHOULDN'T HAVE FIRST DIBS...
BUT MY POOR FATHER GOT PASSED OVER QUICKER THAN YOU CAN SAY "CIGAR!"
WHEN HE FINALLY DID GET TO HOLD ME, THERE WAS LOVE IN HIS SWOLLEN EYES...
HE WRINKLED HIS NOSE AND SMELLED MY LITTLE HEAD...
IT WAS THAT FRESH BABY SMELL THAT HE WOULD NEVER FORGET...

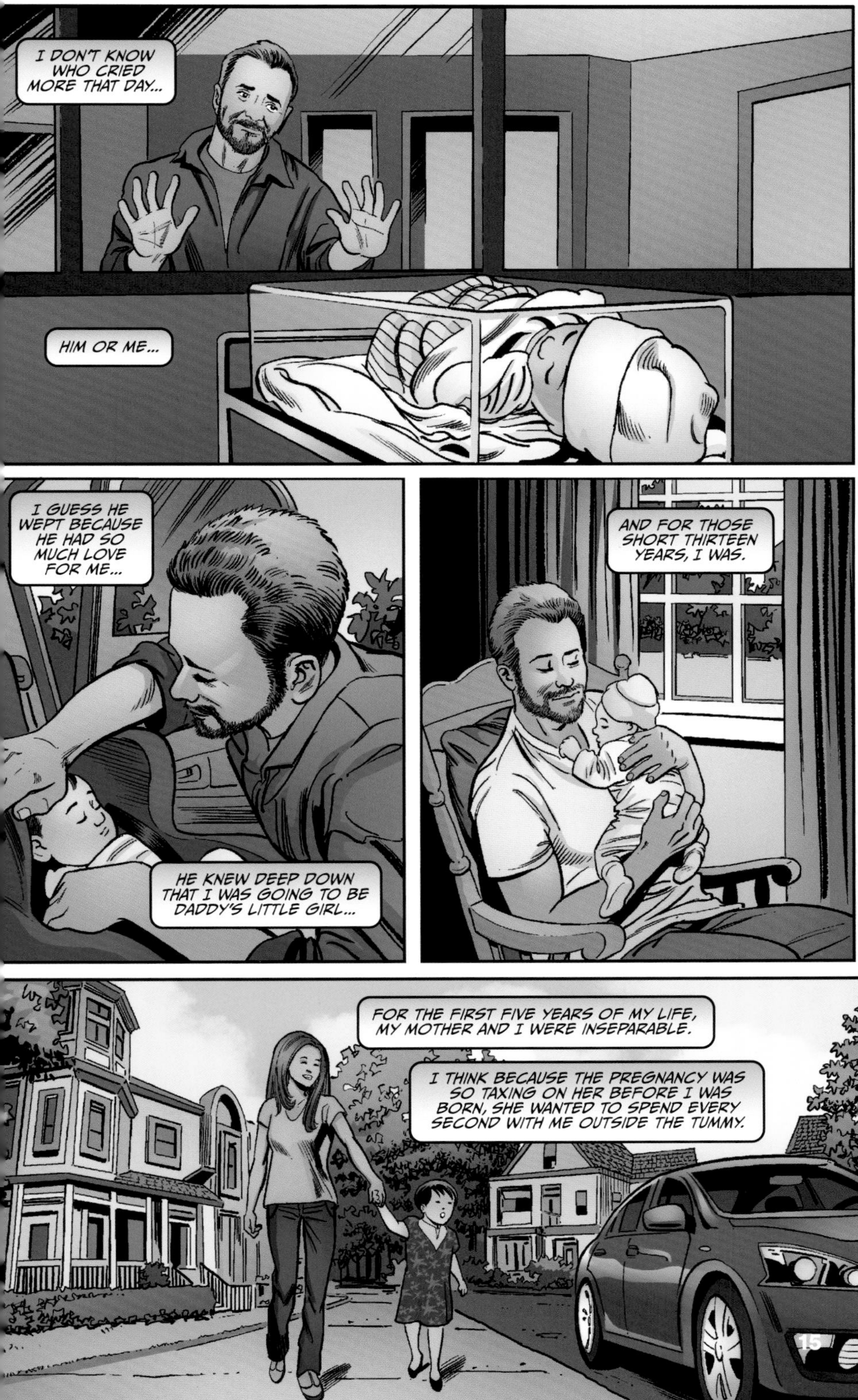

I DON'T KNOW WHO CRIED MORE THAT DAY...
HIM OR ME...
I GUESS HE WEPT BECAUSE HE HAD SO MUCH LOVE FOR ME...
HE KNEW DEEP DOWN THAT I WAS GOING TO BE DADDY'S LITTLE GIRL...
AND FOR THOSE SHORT THIRTEEN YEARS, I WAS.
FOR THE FIRST FIVE YEARS OF MY LIFE, MY MOTHER AND I WERE INSEPARABLE.
I THINK BECAUSE THE PREGNANCY WAS SO TAXING ON HER BEFORE I WAS BORN, SHE WANTED TO SPEND EVERY SECOND WITH ME OUTSIDE THE TUMMY.

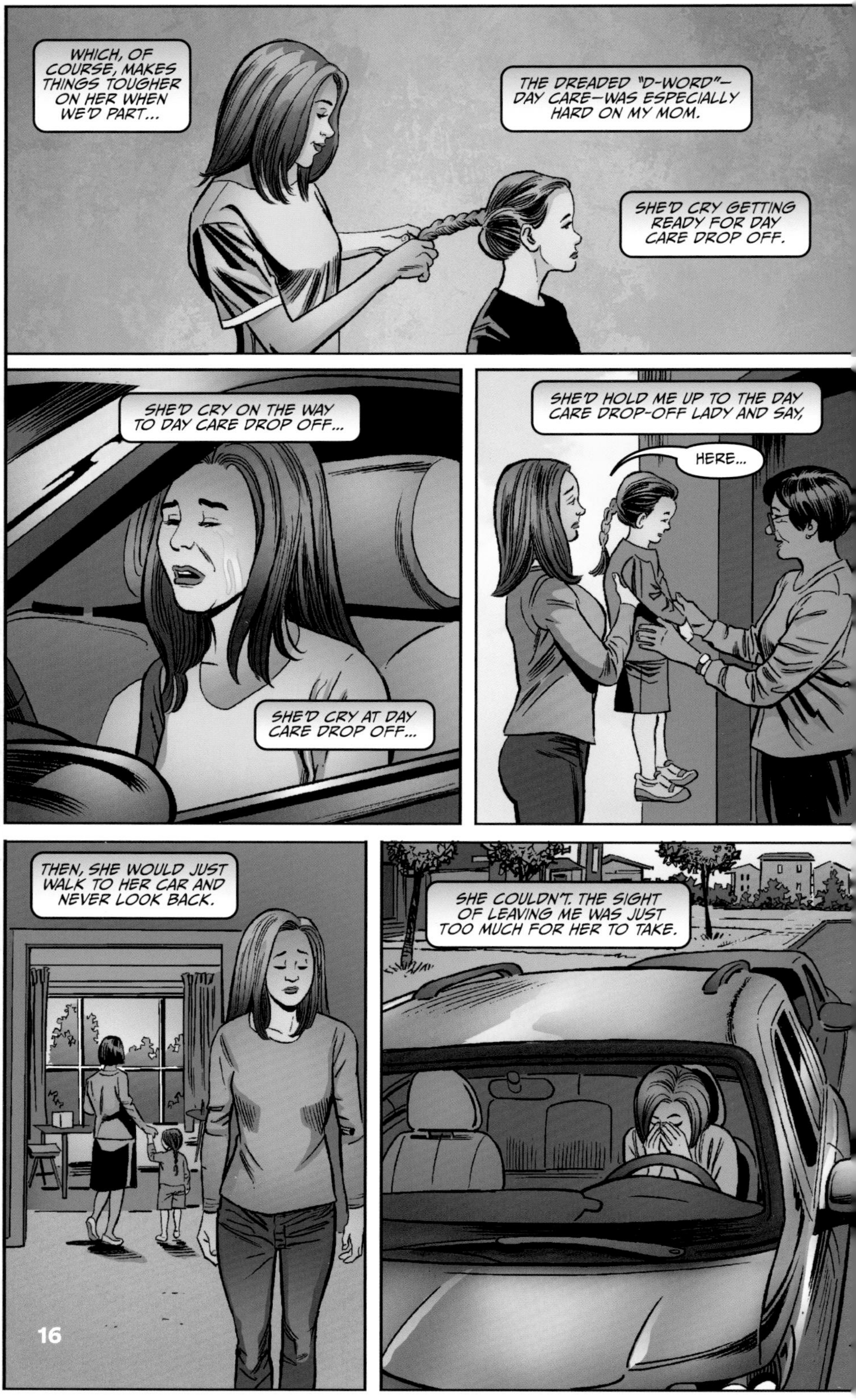

WHICH, OF COURSE, MAKES THINGS TOUGHER ON HER WHEN WE'D PART...
THE DREADED "D-WORD"—DAY CARE—WAS ESPECIALLY HARD ON MY MOM.
SHE'D CRY GETTING READY FOR DAY CARE DROP OFF.
SHE'D CRY ON THE WAY TO DAY CARE DROP OFF...
SHE'D CRY AT DAY CARE DROP OFF...
SHE'D HOLD ME UP TO THE DAY CARE DROP-OFF LADY AND SAY,
HERE...
THEN, SHE WOULD JUST WALK TO HER CAR AND NEVER LOOK BACK.
SHE COULDN'T. THE SIGHT OF LEAVING ME WAS JUST TOO MUCH FOR HER TO TAKE.

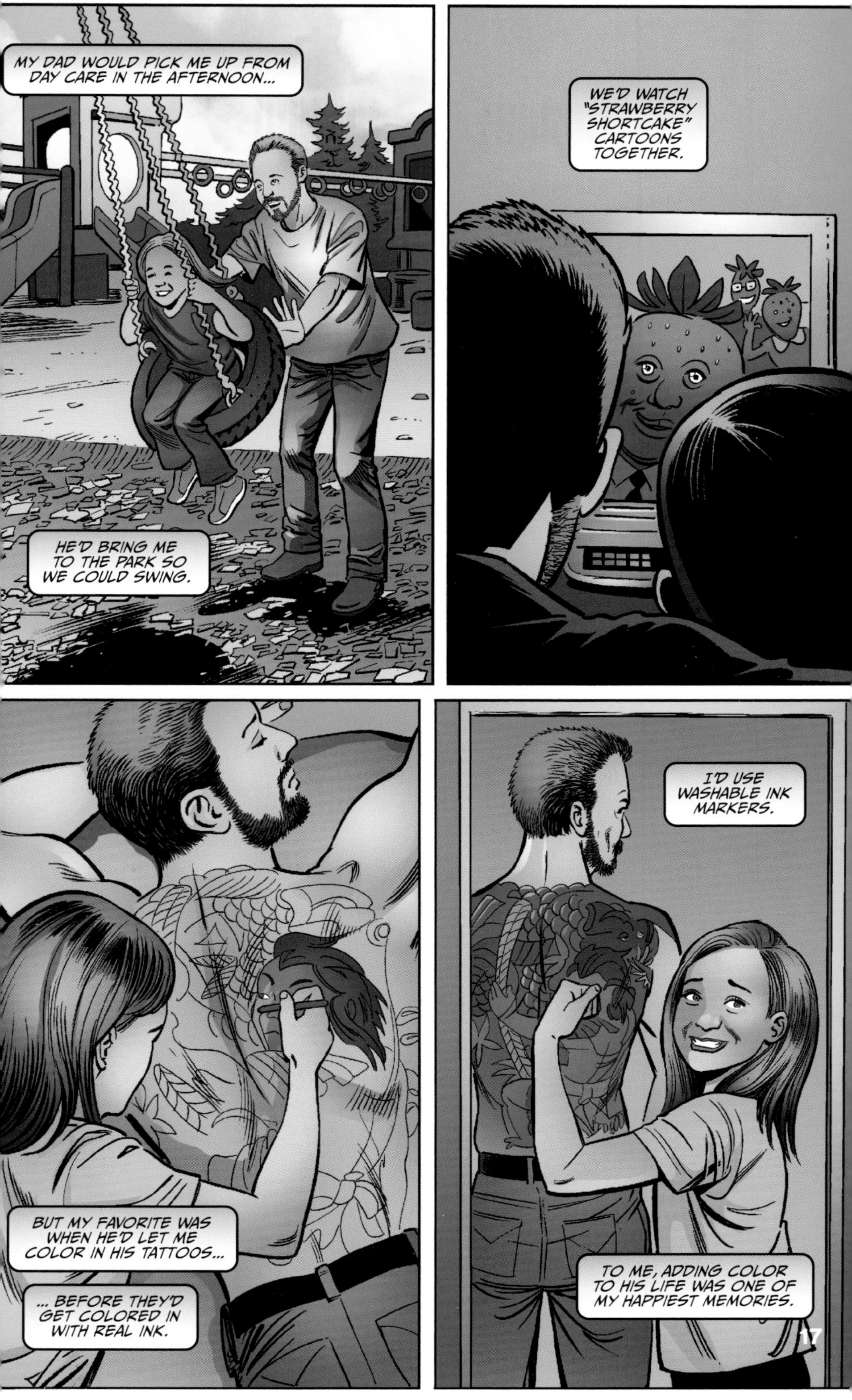
MY DAD WOULD PICK ME UP FROM DAY CARE IN THE AFTERNOON...
HE'D BRING ME TO THE PARK SO WE COULD SWING.
WE'D WATCH "STRAWBERRY SHORTCAKE" CARTOONS TOGETHER.
BUT MY FAVORITE WAS WHEN HE'D LET ME COLOR IN HIS TATTOOS...
... BEFORE THEY'D GET COLORED IN WITH REAL INK.
I'D USE WASHABLE INK MARKERS.
TO ME, ADDING COLOR TO HIS LIFE WAS ONE OF MY HAPPIEST MEMORIES.

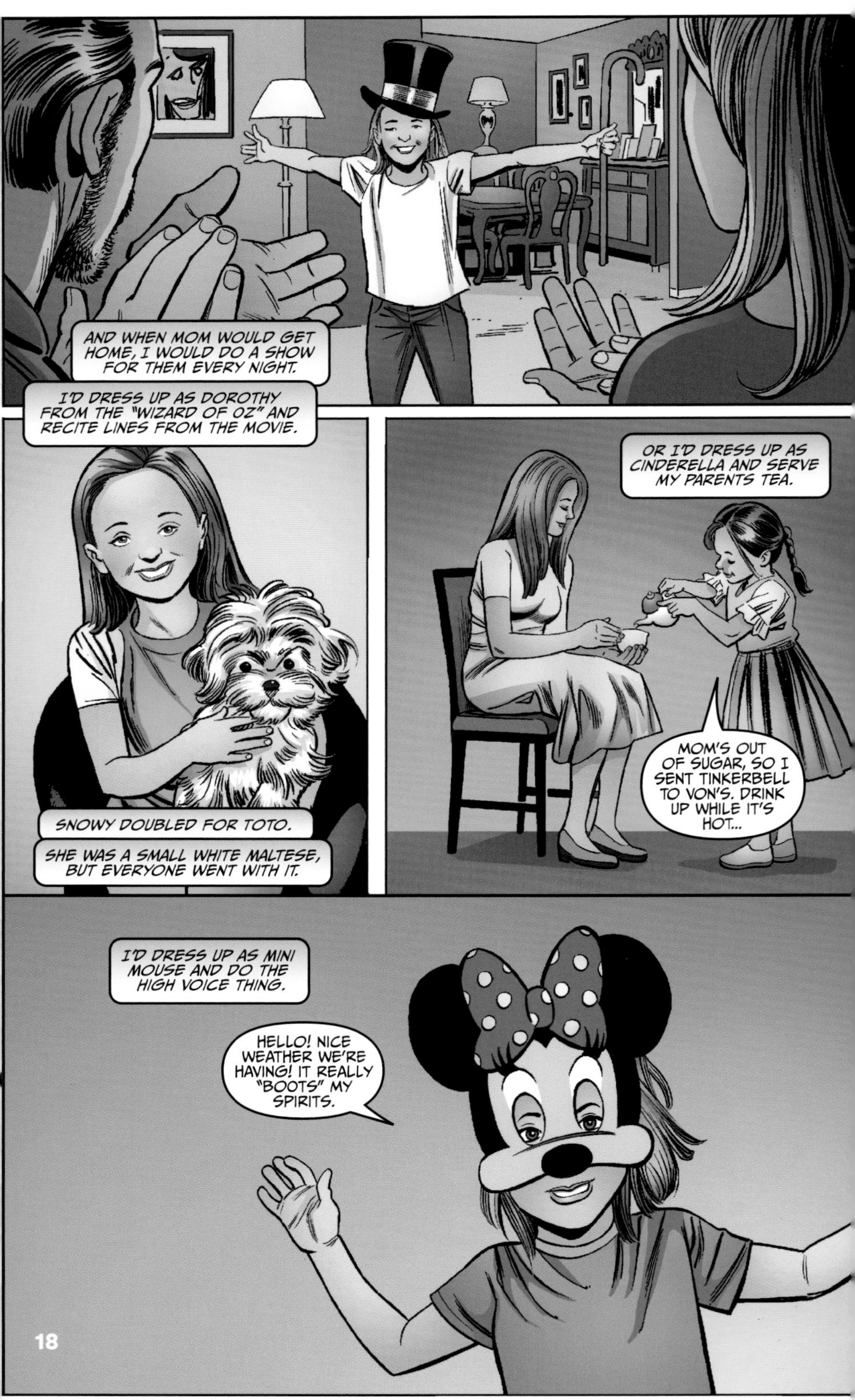
AND WHEN MOM WOULD GET HOME, I WOULD DO A SHOW FOR THEM EVERY NIGHT.
I'D DRESS UP AS DOROTHY FROM THE "WIZARD OF OZ" AND RECITE LINES FROM THE MOVIE.
SNOWY DOUBLED FOR TOTO.
SHE WAS A SMALL WHITE MALTESE, BUT EVERYONE WENT WITH IT.
OR I'D DRESS UP AS CINDERELLA AND SERVE MY PARENTS TEA.
MOM'S OUT OF SUGAR, SO I SENT TINKERBELL TO VON'S. DRINK UP WHILE IT'S HOT...
I'D DRESS UP AS MINI MOUSE AND DO THE HIGH VOICE THING.
HELLO! NICE WEATHER WE'RE HAVING! IT REALLY "BOOTS" MY SPIRITS.

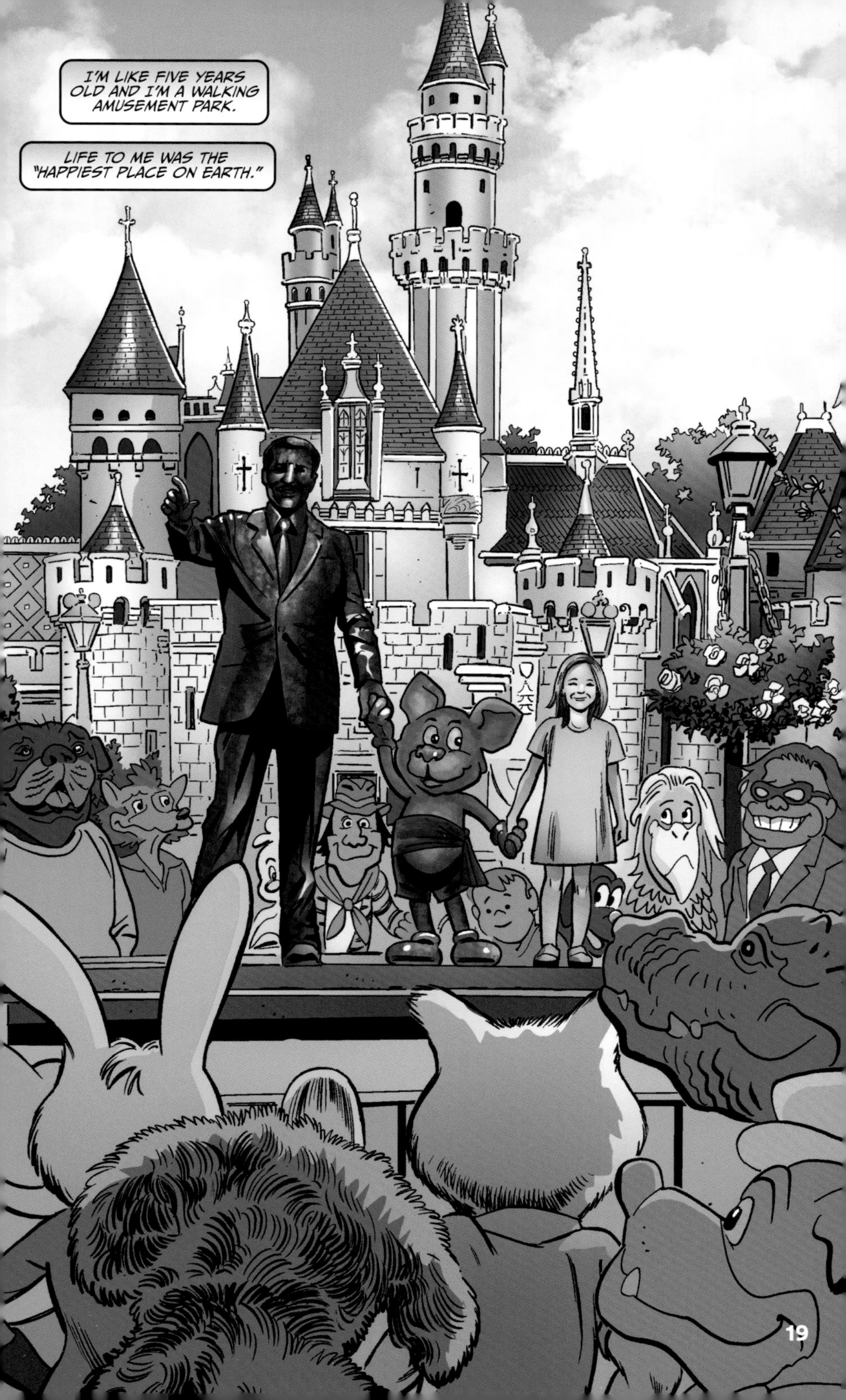
I'M LIKE FIVE YEARS OLD AND I'M A WALKING AMUSEMENT PARK.
LIFE TO ME WAS THE "HAPPIEST PLACE ON EARTH."

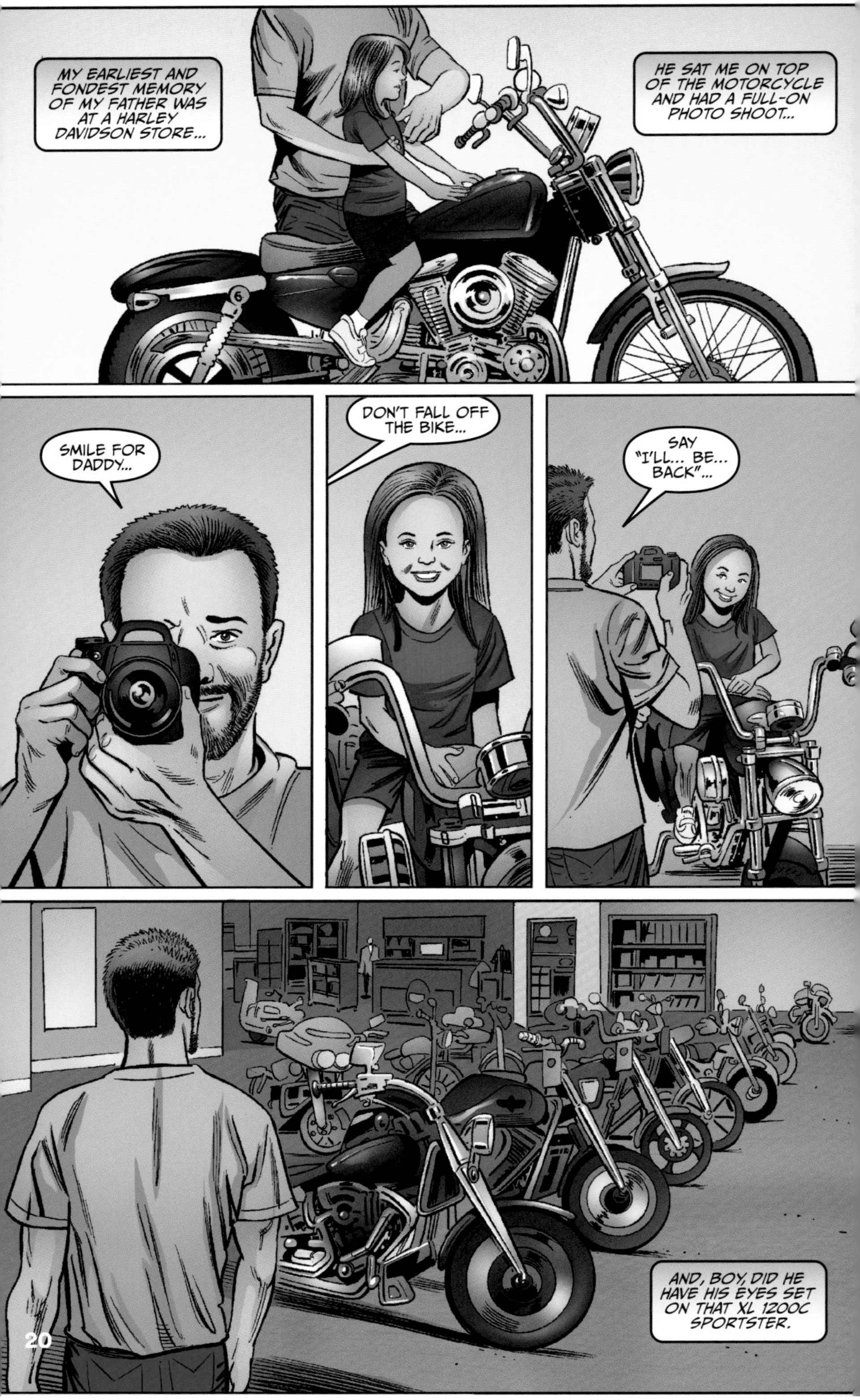
MY EARLIEST AND FONDEST MEMORY OF MY FATHER WAS AT A HARLEY DAVIDSON STORE...
HE SAT ME ON TOP OF THE MOTORCYCLE AND HAD A FULL-ON PHOTO SHOOT...
SMILE FOR DADDY...
DON'T FALL OFF THE BIKE...
SAY "I'LL... BE... BACK"...
AND, BOY, DID HE HAVE HIS EYES SET ON THAT XL 1200C SPORTSTER.

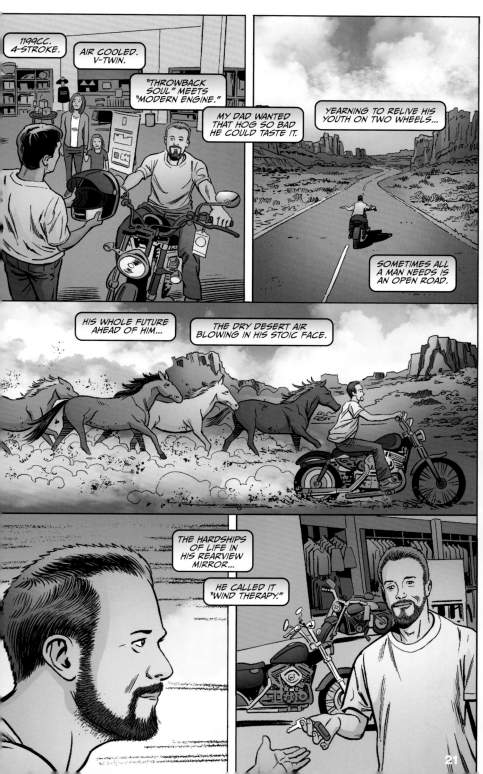

1199CC. 4-STROKE.

AIR COOLED. V-TWIN.

"THROWBACK SOUL" MEETS "MODERN ENGINE."

MY DAD WANTED THAT HOG SO BAD HE COULD TASTE IT.

YEARNING TO RELIVE HIS YOUTH ON TWO WHEELS...

SOMETIMES ALL A MAN NEEDS IS AN OPEN ROAD.

HIS WHOLE FUTURE AHEAD OF HIM...

THE DRY DESERT AIR BLOWING IN HIS STOIC FACE.

THE HARDSHIPS OF LIFE IN HIS REARVIEW MIRROR...

HE CALLED IT "WIND THERAPY."

WELL, MY MOTHER PUT THE BRAKES ON THAT DREAM WITH ONE SIMPLE STATEMENT...

INSERT THICK BROOKLYN ACCENT--

YOU CAN GET THAT CYCLE, BUT...

THERE'S A STRONG POSSIBILITY I'M PREGNANT AGAIN.

IF I'M NOT PREGNANT, THE BIKE IS YOURS...

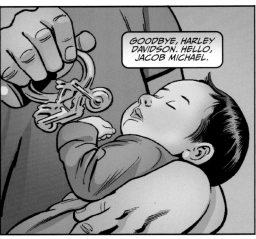

GOODBYE, HARLEY DAVIDSON. HELLO, JACOB MICHAEL.

I REMEMBER RUNNING AROUND THE HOUSE SINGING,

MOMMY'S HAVING A BABY... MOMMY'S HAVING A BABY...

SO, UNFORTUNATELY, FOR MY DAD...

HE LOST THE SUN... FOR A SON...

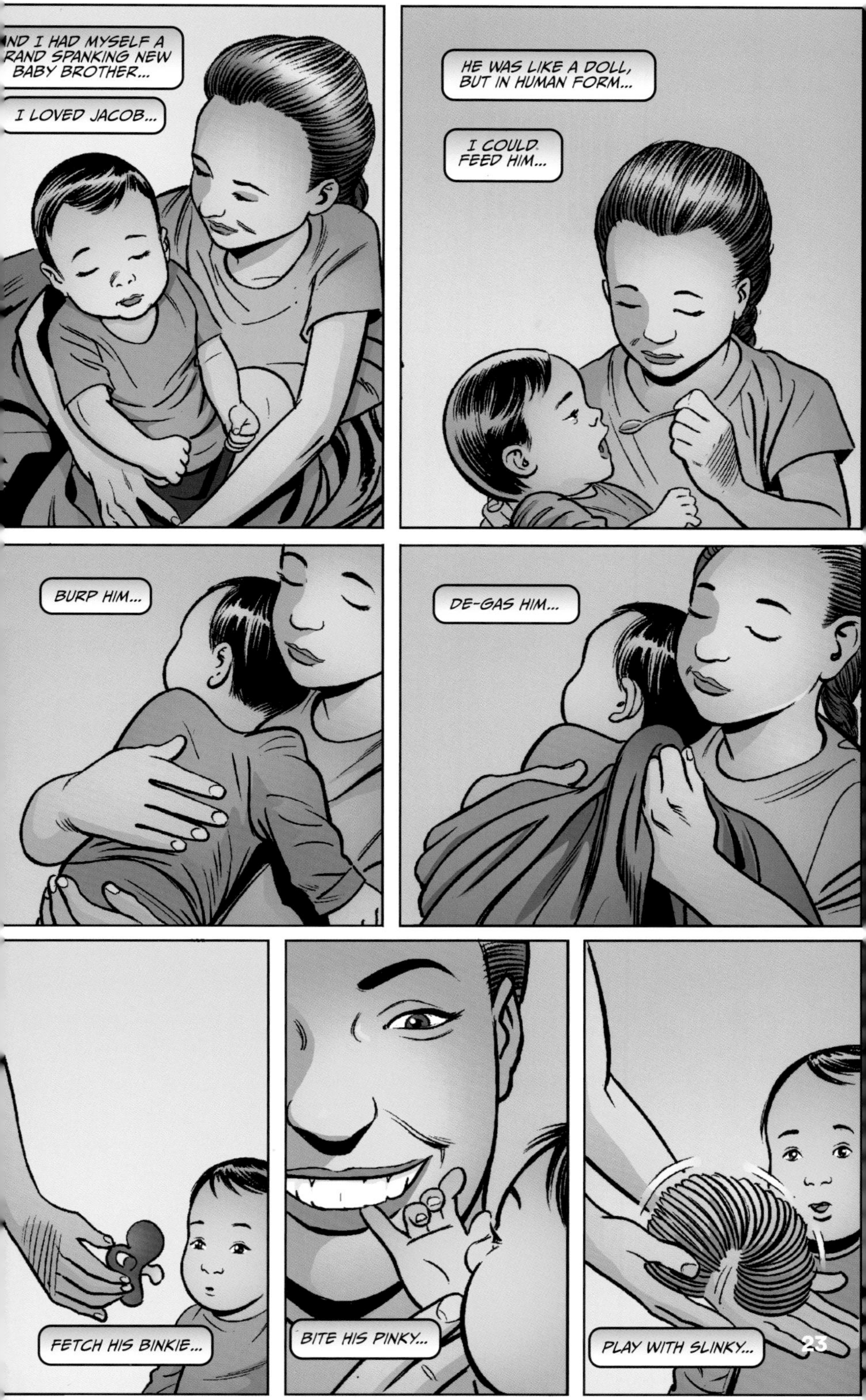
ND I HAD MYSELF A RAND SPANKING NEW BABY BROTHER...
I LOVED JACOB...
HE WAS LIKE A DOLL, BUT IN HUMAN FORM...
I COULD FEED HIM...
BURP HIM...
DE-GAS HIM...
FETCH HIS BINKIE...
BITE HIS PINKY...
PLAY WITH SLINKY...

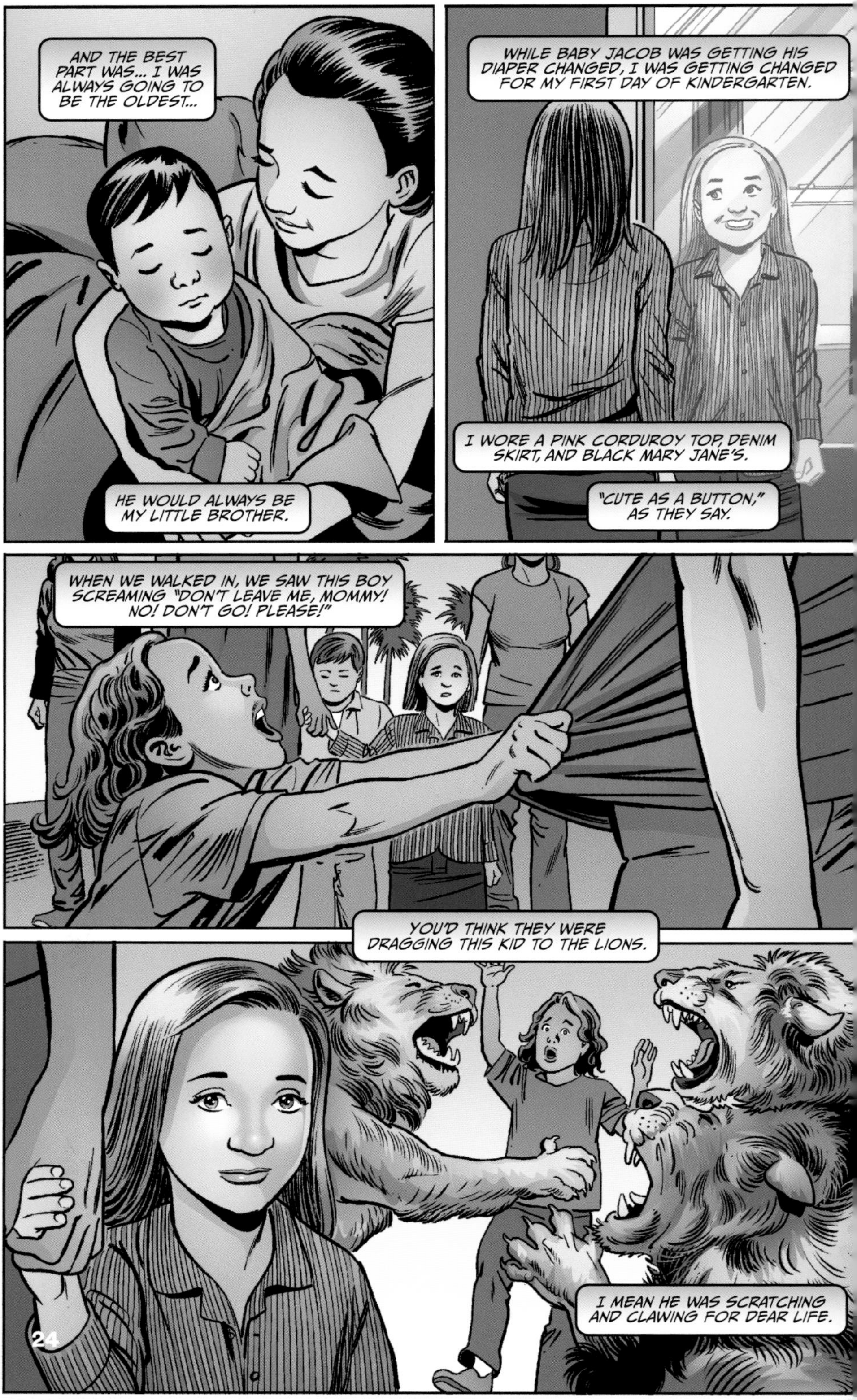
AND THE BEST PART WAS... I WAS ALWAYS GOING TO BE THE OLDEST...
HE WOULD ALWAYS BE MY LITTLE BROTHER.
WHILE BABY JACOB WAS GETTING HIS DIAPER CHANGED, I WAS GETTING CHANGED FOR MY FIRST DAY OF KINDERGARTEN.
I WORE A PINK CORDUROY TOP, DENIM SKIRT, AND BLACK MARY JANE'S.
"CUTE AS A BUTTON," AS THEY SAY.
WHEN WE WALKED IN, WE SAW THIS BOY SCREAMING "DON'T LEAVE ME, MOMMY! NO! DON'T GO! PLEASE!"
YOU'D THINK THEY WERE DRAGGING THIS KID TO THE LIONS.
I MEAN HE WAS SCRATCHING AND CLAWING FOR DEAR LIFE.
24

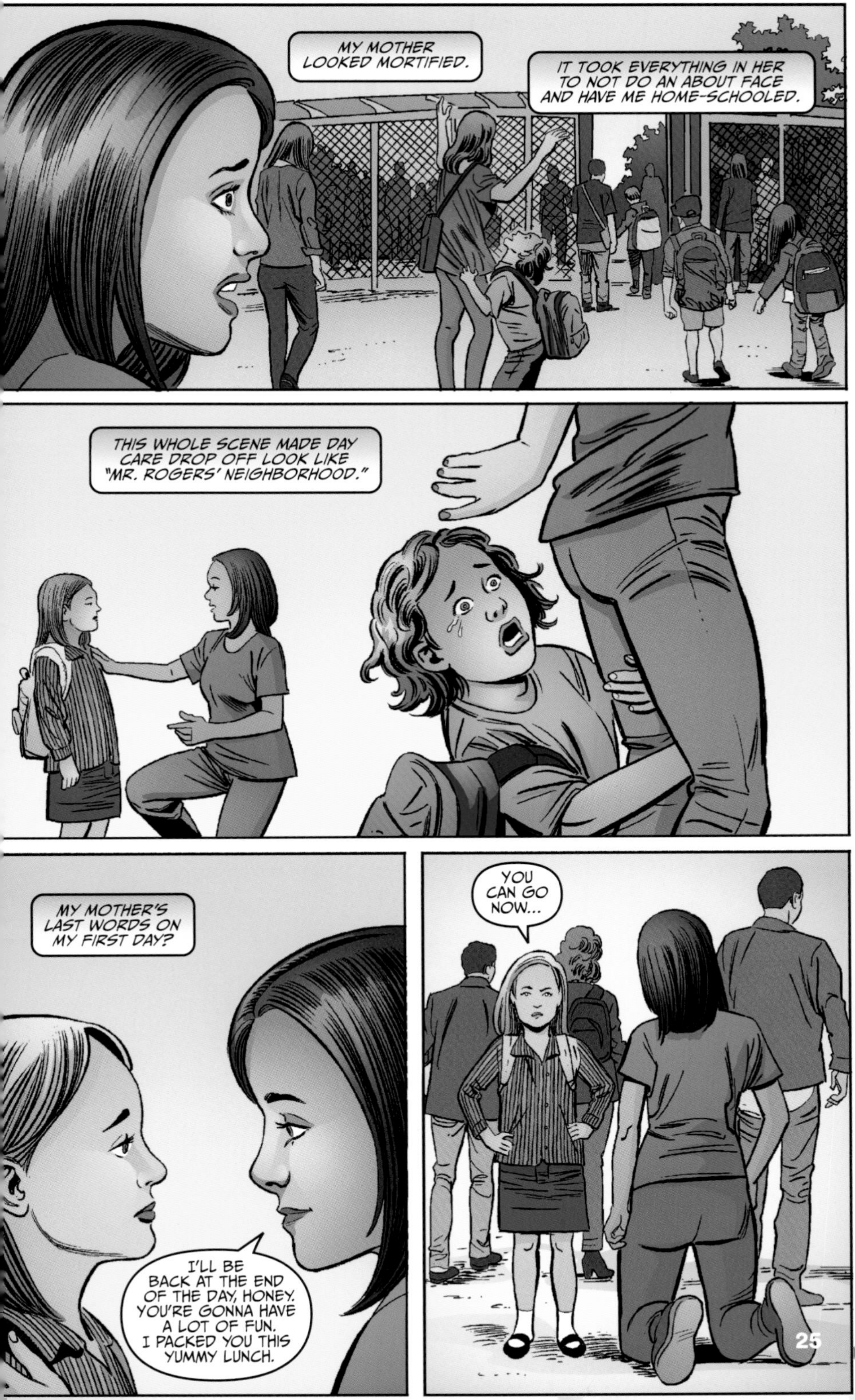

MY MOTHER LOOKED MORTIFIED.
IT TOOK EVERYTHING IN HER TO NOT DO AN ABOUT FACE AND HAVE ME HOME-SCHOOLED.
THIS WHOLE SCENE MADE DAY CARE DROP OFF LOOK LIKE "MR. ROGERS' NEIGHBORHOOD."
MY MOTHER'S LAST WORDS ON MY FIRST DAY?
I'LL BE BACK AT THE END OF THE DAY, HONEY. YOU'RE GONNA HAVE A LOT OF FUN. I PACKED YOU THIS YUMMY LUNCH.
YOU CAN GO NOW...

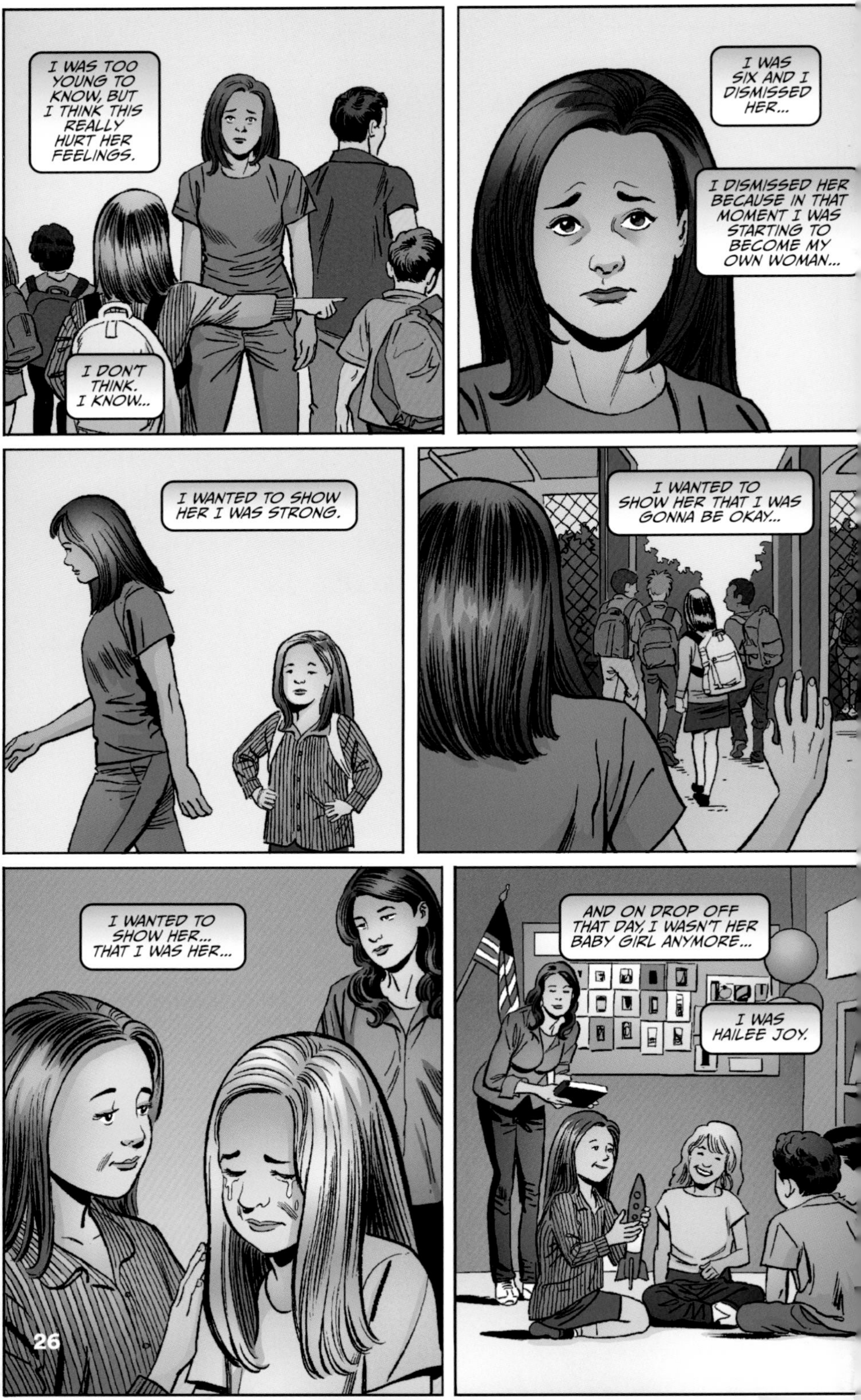
I WAS TOO YOUNG TO KNOW, BUT I THINK THIS REALLY HURT HER FEELINGS.
I DON'T THINK. I KNOW...
I WAS SIX AND I DISMISSED HER...
I DISMISSED HER BECAUSE IN THAT MOMENT I WAS STARTING TO BECOME MY OWN WOMAN...
I WANTED TO SHOW HER I WAS STRONG.
I WANTED TO SHOW HER THAT I WAS GONNA BE OKAY...
I WANTED TO SHOW HER... THAT I WAS HER...
AND ON DROP OFF THAT DAY, I WASN'T HER BABY GIRL ANYMORE...
I WAS HAILEE JOY.

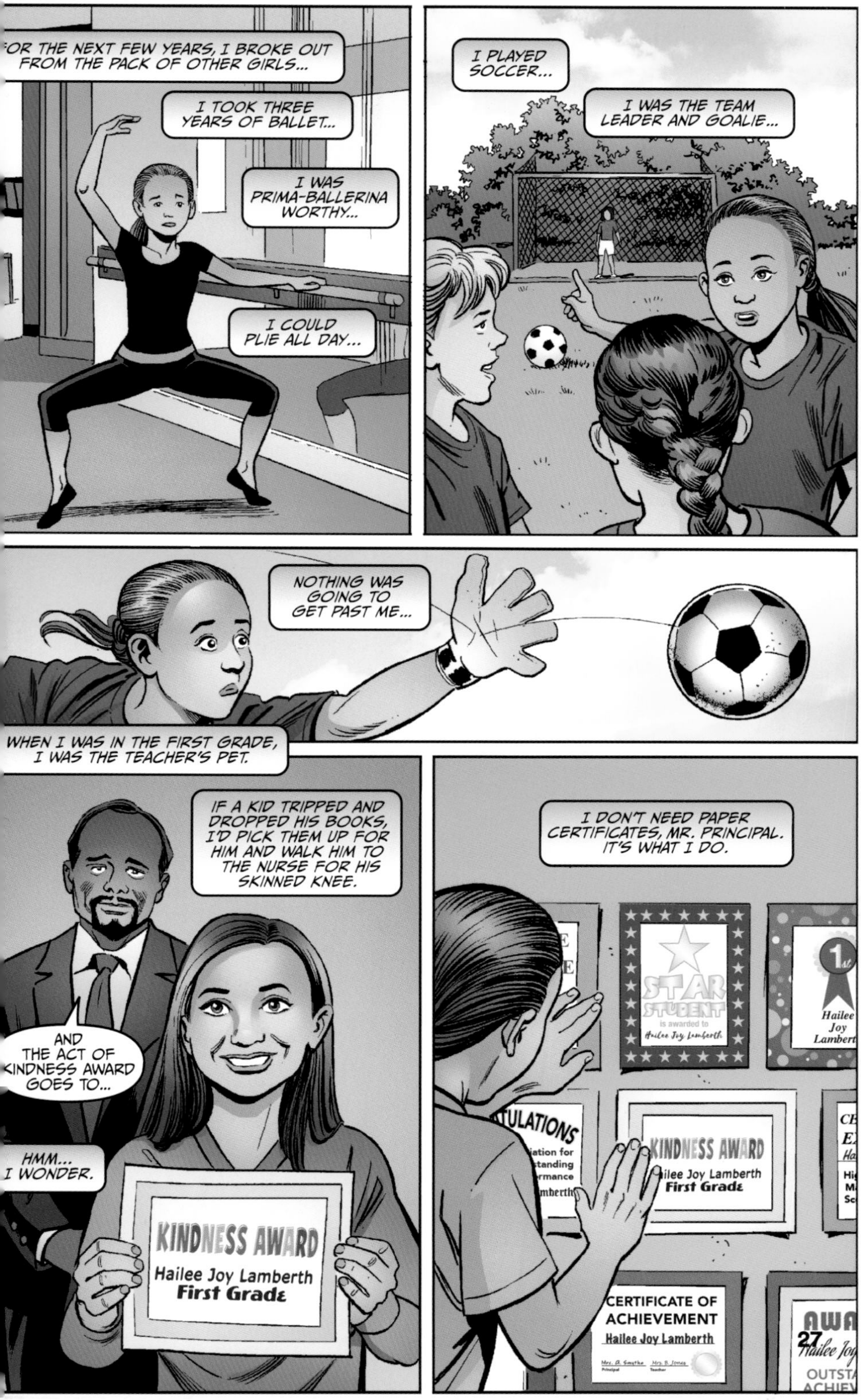

FOR THE NEXT FEW YEARS, I BROKE OUT FROM THE PACK OF OTHER GIRLS...
I TOOK THREE YEARS OF BALLET...
I WAS PRIMA-BALLERINA WORTHY...
I COULD PLIE ALL DAY...
I PLAYED SOCCER...
I WAS THE TEAM LEADER AND GOALIE...
NOTHING WAS GOING TO GET PAST ME...
WHEN I WAS IN THE FIRST GRADE, I WAS THE TEACHER'S PET.
IF A KID TRIPPED AND DROPPED HIS BOOKS, I'D PICK THEM UP FOR HIM AND WALK HIM TO THE NURSE FOR HIS SKINNED KNEE.
AND THE ACT OF KINDNESS AWARD GOES TO...
HMM... I WONDER.
KINDNESS AWARD
Hailee Joy Lamberth
First Grade
I DON'T NEED PAPER CERTIFICATES, MR. PRINCIPAL. IT'S WHAT I DO.
STAR STUDENT
is awarded to
Hailee Joy Lamberth
Hailee Joy Lambert
KINDNESS AWARD
ailee Joy Lamberth
First Grade
CERTIFICATE OF ACHIEVEMENT
Hailee Joy Lamberth

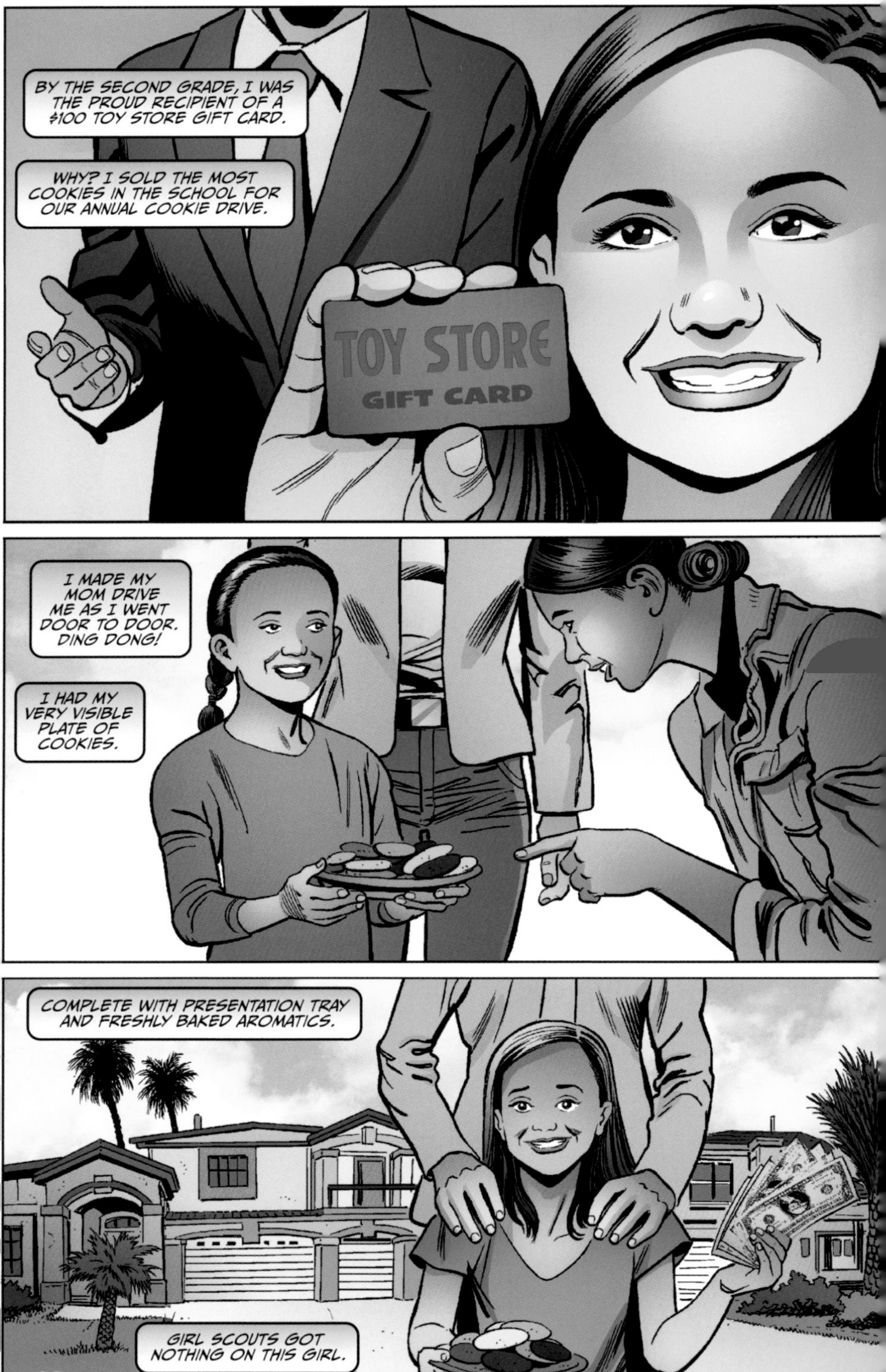
BY THE SECOND GRADE, I WAS THE PROUD RECIPIENT OF A $100 TOY STORE GIFT CARD.
WHY? I SOLD THE MOST COOKIES IN THE SCHOOL FOR OUR ANNUAL COOKIE DRIVE.
TOY STORE
GIFT CARD
I MADE MY MOM DRIVE ME AS I WENT DOOR TO DOOR. DING DONG!
I HAD MY VERY VISIBLE PLATE OF COOKIES.
COMPLETE WITH PRESENTATION TRAY AND FRESHLY BAKED AROMATICS.
GIRL SCOUTS GOT NOTHING ON THIS GIRL.

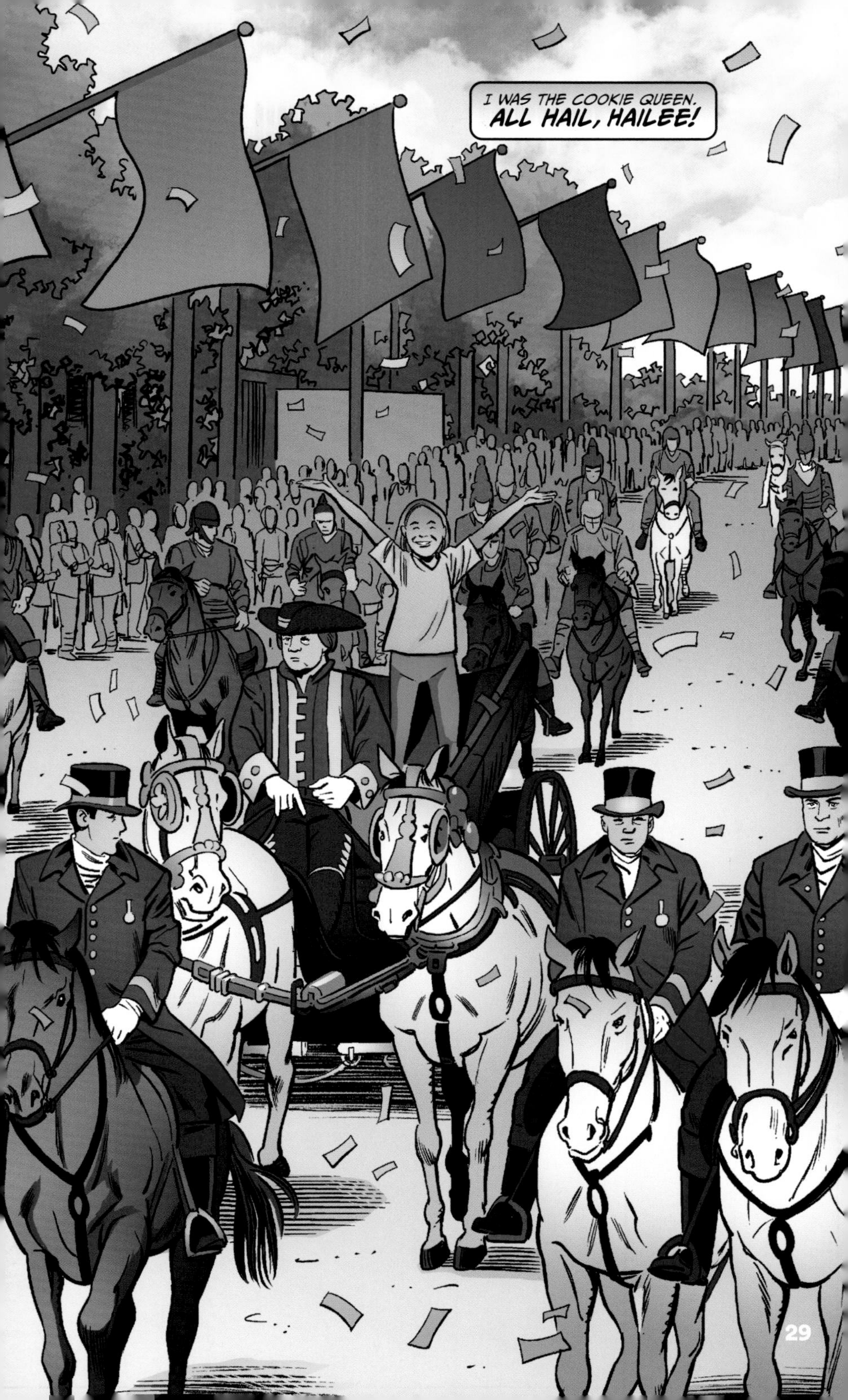
I WAS THE COOKIE QUEEN.
ALL HAIL, HAILEE!

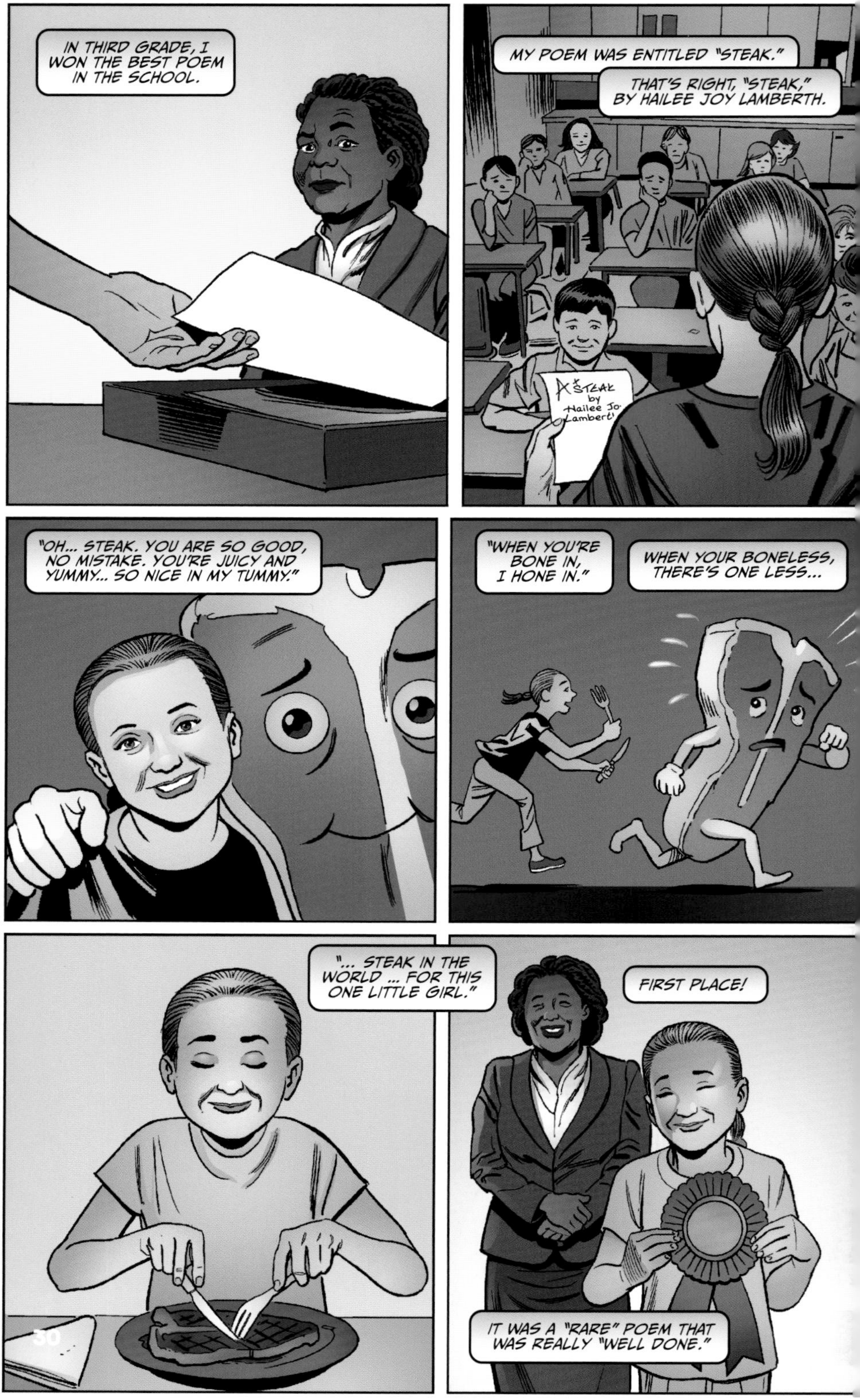
IN THIRD GRADE, I WON THE BEST POEM IN THE SCHOOL.
MY POEM WAS ENTITLED "STEAK."
THAT'S RIGHT, "STEAK," BY HAILEE JOY LAMBERTH.
A+ STEAK by Hailee Jo Lambert
"OH... STEAK. YOU ARE SO GOOD, NO MISTAKE. YOU'RE JUICY AND YUMMY... SO NICE IN MY TUMMY."
"WHEN YOU'RE BONE IN, I HONE IN."
WHEN YOUR BONELESS, THERE'S ONE LESS...
"... STEAK IN THE WORLD ... FOR THIS ONE LITTLE GIRL."
FIRST PLACE!
IT WAS A "RARE" POEM THAT WAS REALLY "WELL DONE."

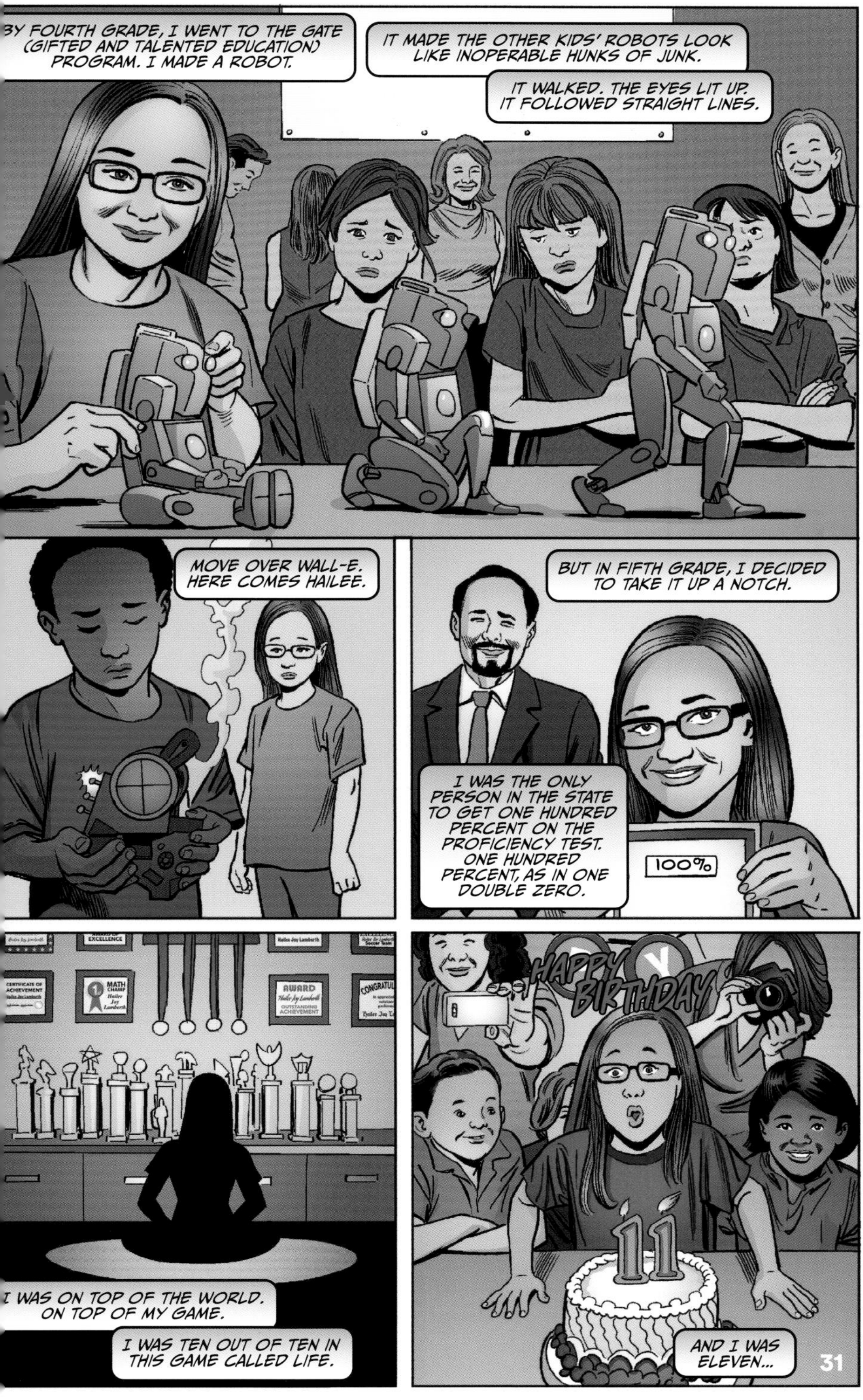
BY FOURTH GRADE, I WENT TO THE GATE (GIFTED AND TALENTED EDUCATION) PROGRAM. I MADE A ROBOT.
IT MADE THE OTHER KIDS' ROBOTS LOOK LIKE INOPERABLE HUNKS OF JUNK.
IT WALKED. THE EYES LIT UP. IT FOLLOWED STRAIGHT LINES.
MOVE OVER WALL-E. HERE COMES HAILEE.
BUT IN FIFTH GRADE, I DECIDED TO TAKE IT UP A NOTCH.
I WAS THE ONLY PERSON IN THE STATE TO GET ONE HUNDRED PERCENT ON THE PROFICIENCY TEST. ONE HUNDRED PERCENT, AS IN ONE DOUBLE ZERO.
100%
EXCELLENCE
CERTIFICATE OF ACHIEVEMENT
MATH CHAMP
AWARD
OUTSTANDING ACHIEVEMENT
CONGRATUL
I WAS ON TOP OF THE WORLD. ON TOP OF MY GAME.
I WAS TEN OUT OF TEN IN THIS GAME CALLED LIFE.
HAPPY BIRTHDAY
11
AND I WAS ELEVEN...

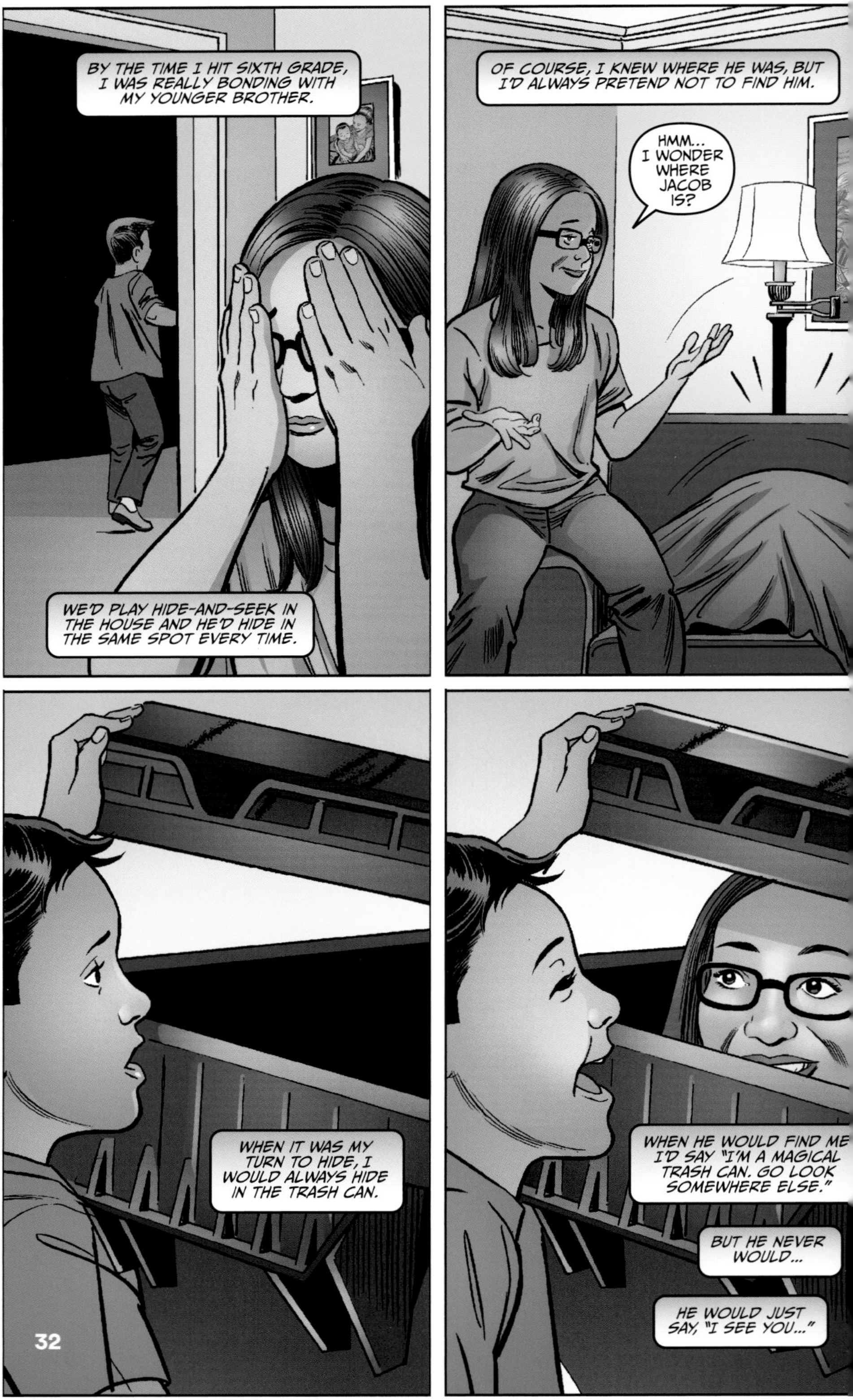
BY THE TIME I HIT SIXTH GRADE, I WAS REALLY BONDING WITH MY YOUNGER BROTHER.
WE'D PLAY HIDE-AND-SEEK IN THE HOUSE AND HE'D HIDE IN THE SAME SPOT EVERY TIME.
OF COURSE, I KNEW WHERE HE WAS, BUT I'D ALWAYS PRETEND NOT TO FIND HIM.
HMM... I WONDER WHERE JACOB IS?
WHEN IT WAS MY TURN TO HIDE, I WOULD ALWAYS HIDE IN THE TRASH CAN.
WHEN HE WOULD FIND ME I'D SAY "I'M A MAGICAL TRASH CAN. GO LOOK SOMEWHERE ELSE."
BUT HE NEVER WOULD...
HE WOULD JUST SAY, "I SEE YOU..."

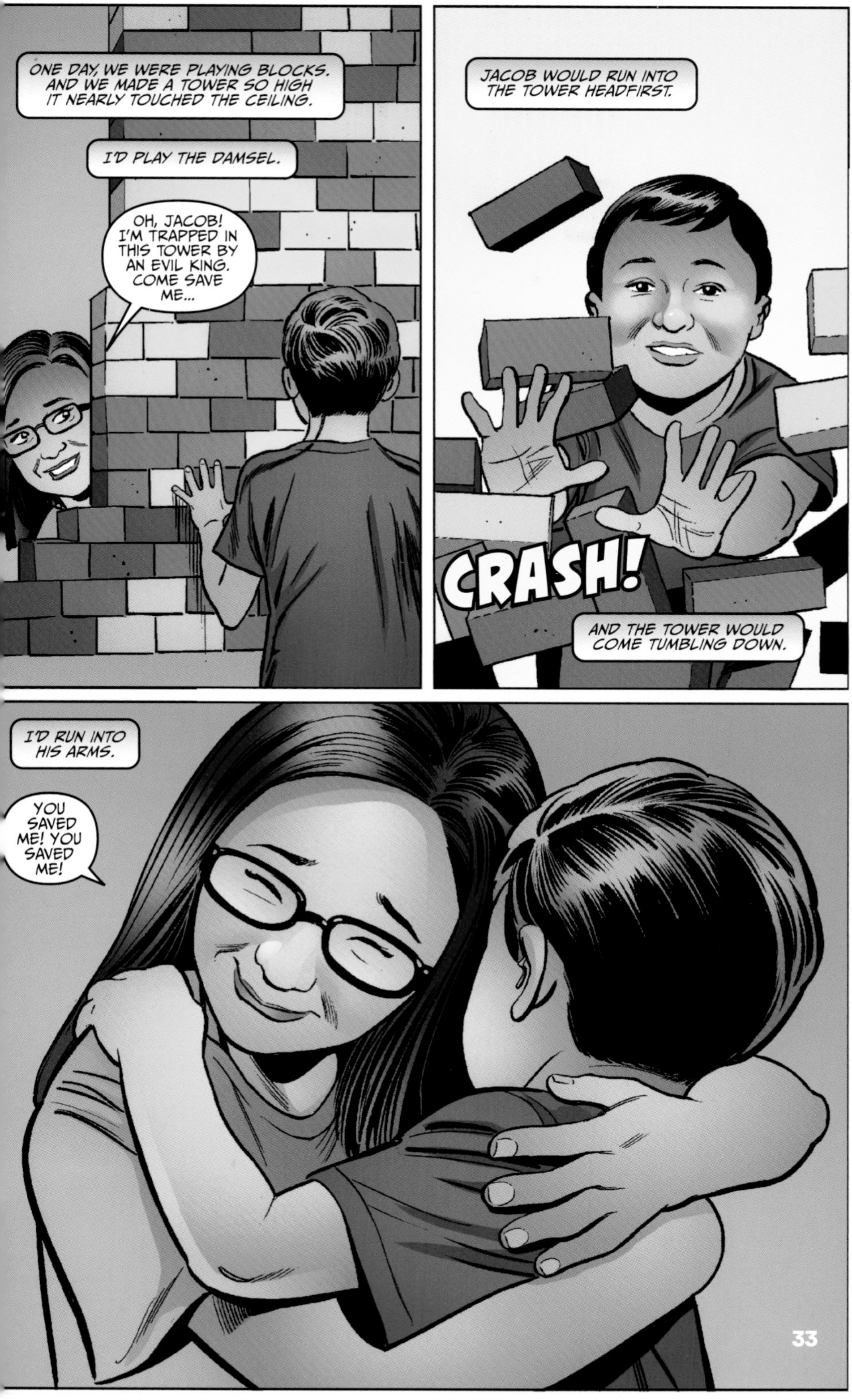
ONE DAY, WE WERE PLAYING BLOCKS. AND WE MADE A TOWER SO HIGH IT NEARLY TOUCHED THE CEILING.
I'D PLAY THE DAMSEL.
OH, JACOB! I'M TRAPPED IN THIS TOWER BY AN EVIL KING. COME SAVE ME...
JACOB WOULD RUN INTO THE TOWER HEADFIRST.
CRASH!
AND THE TOWER WOULD COME TUMBLING DOWN.
I'D RUN INTO HIS ARMS.
YOU SAVED ME! YOU SAVED ME!

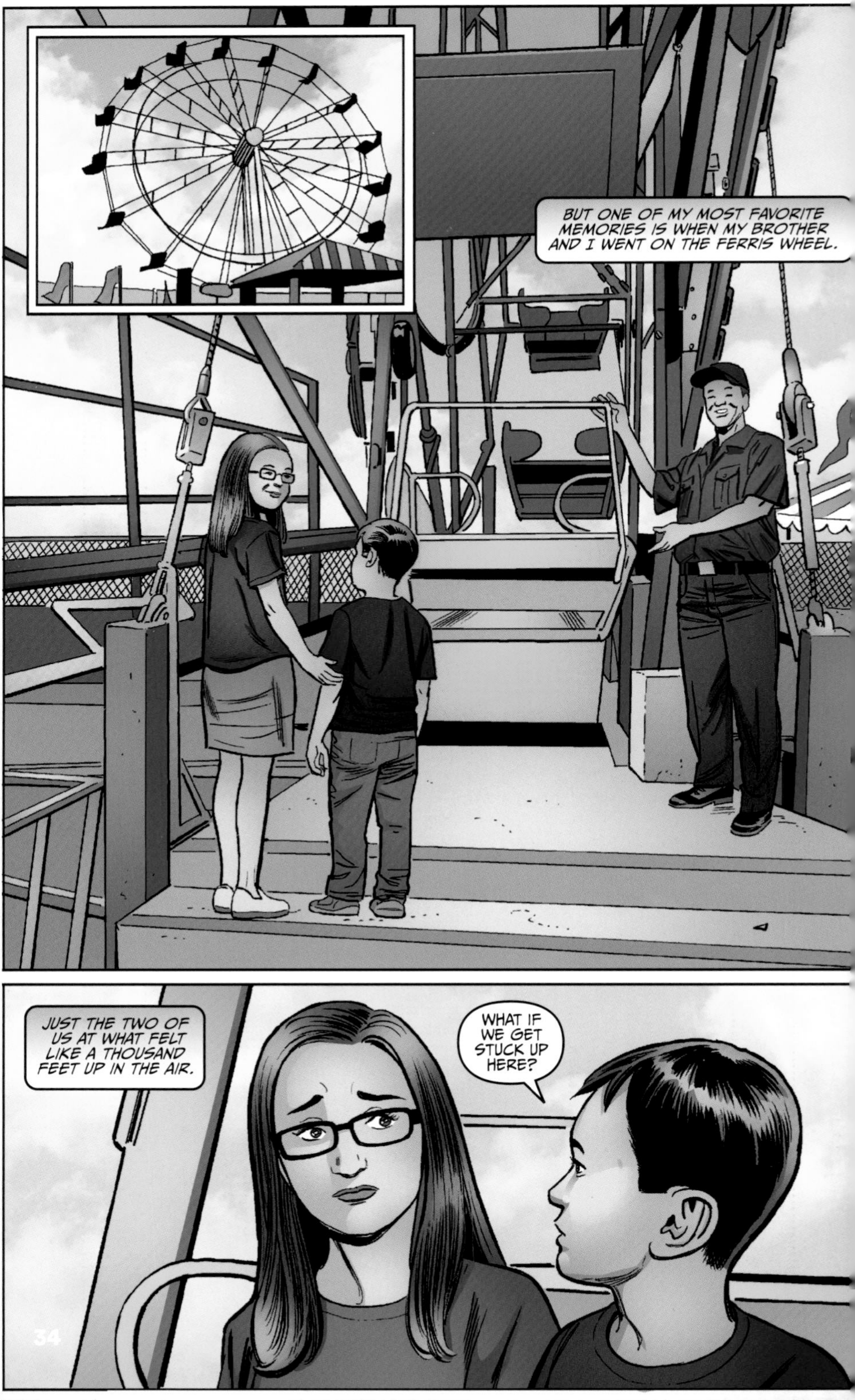
BUT ONE OF MY MOST FAVORITE MEMORIES IS WHEN MY BROTHER AND I WENT ON THE FERRIS WHEEL.
JUST THE TWO OF US AT WHAT FELT LIKE A THOUSAND FEET UP IN THE AIR.
WHAT IF WE GET STUCK UP HERE?

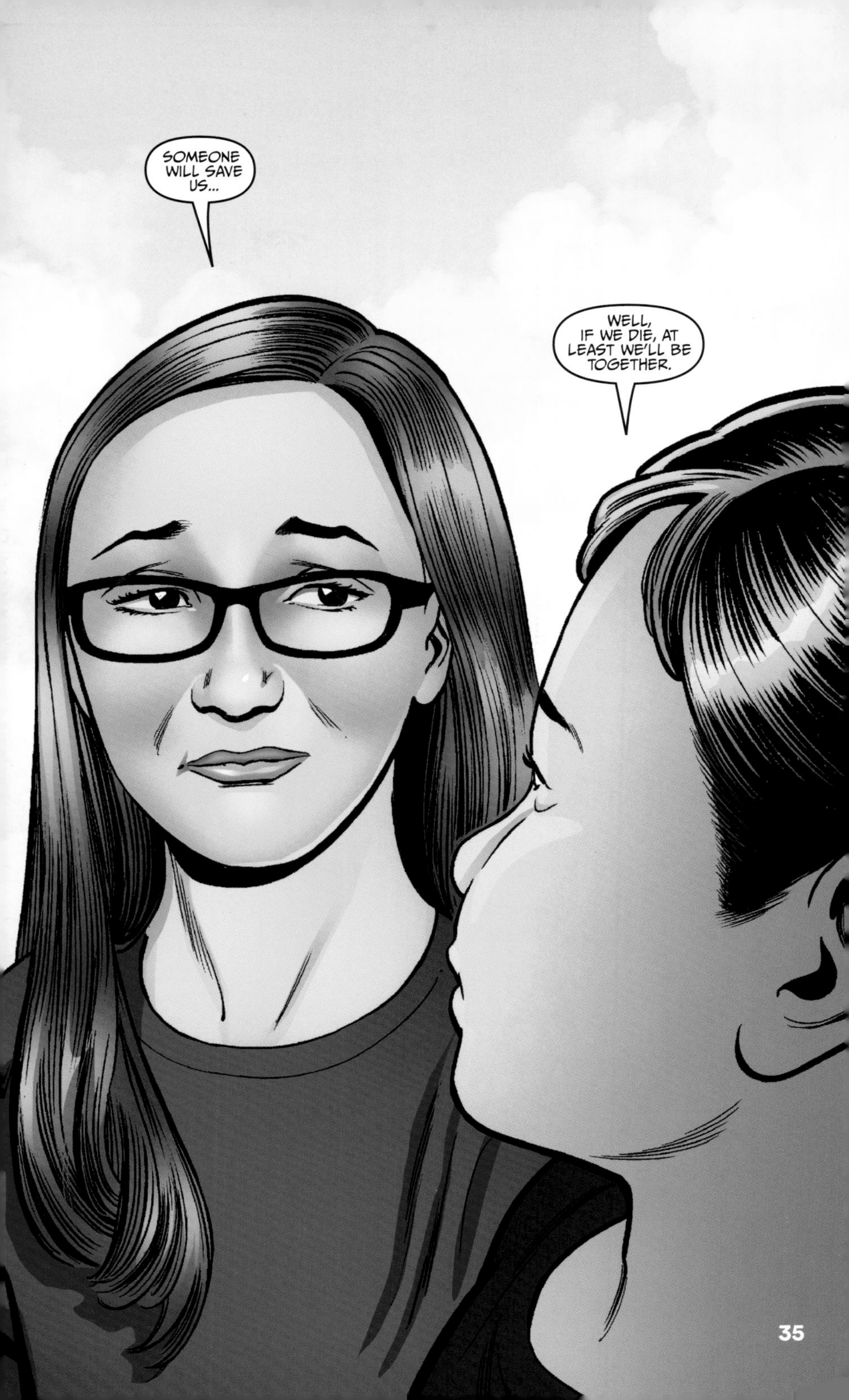
SOMEONE WILL SAVE US...
WELL, IF WE DIE, AT LEAST WE'LL BE TOGETHER.

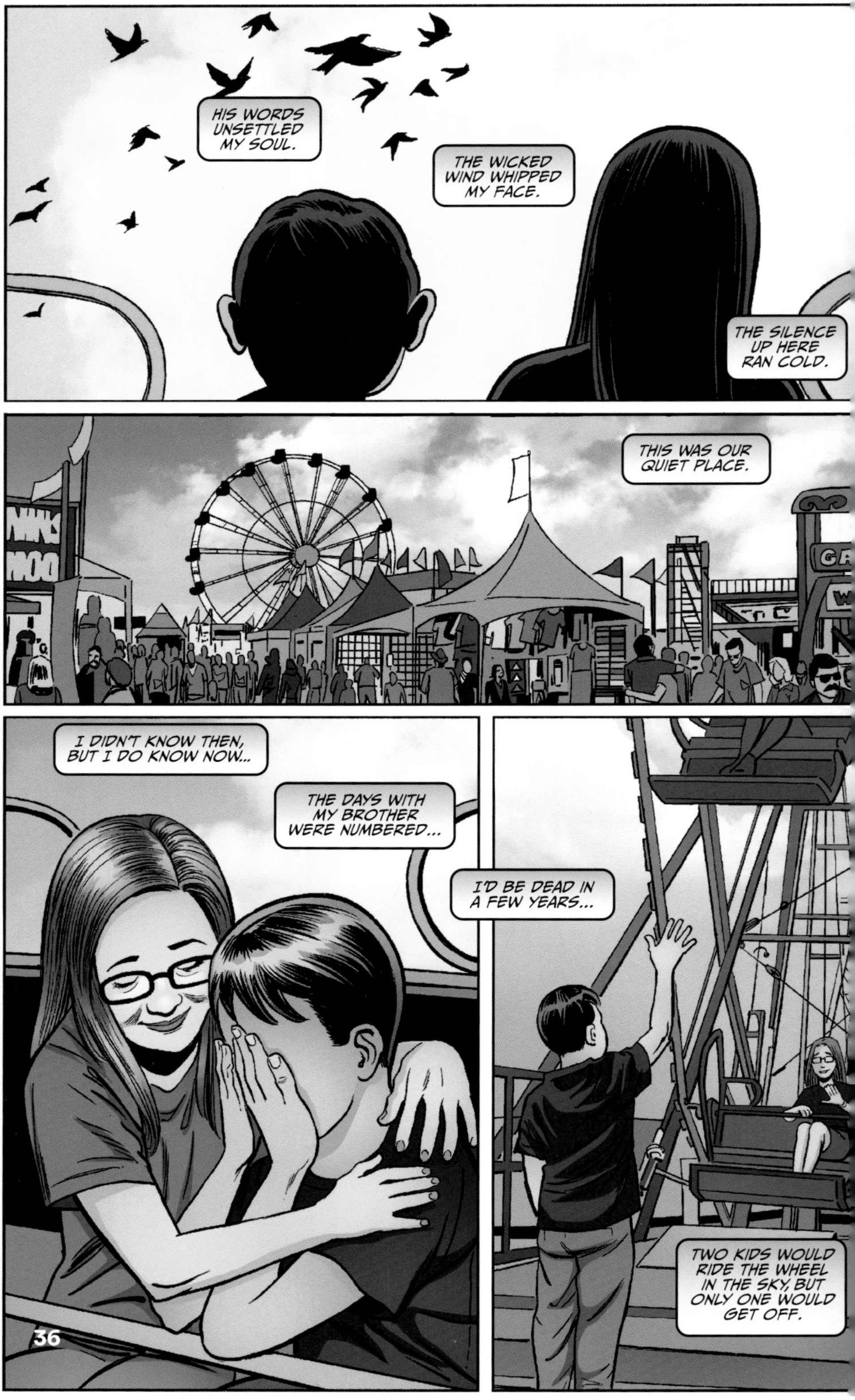
HIS WORDS UNSETTLED MY SOUL.
THE WICKED WIND WHIPPED MY FACE.
THE SILENCE UP HERE RAN COLD.
THIS WAS OUR QUIET PLACE.
I DIDN'T KNOW THEN, BUT I DO KNOW NOW...
THE DAYS WITH MY BROTHER WERE NUMBERED...
I'D BE DEAD IN A FEW YEARS...
TWO KIDS WOULD RIDE THE WHEEL IN THE SKY, BUT ONLY ONE WOULD GET OFF.

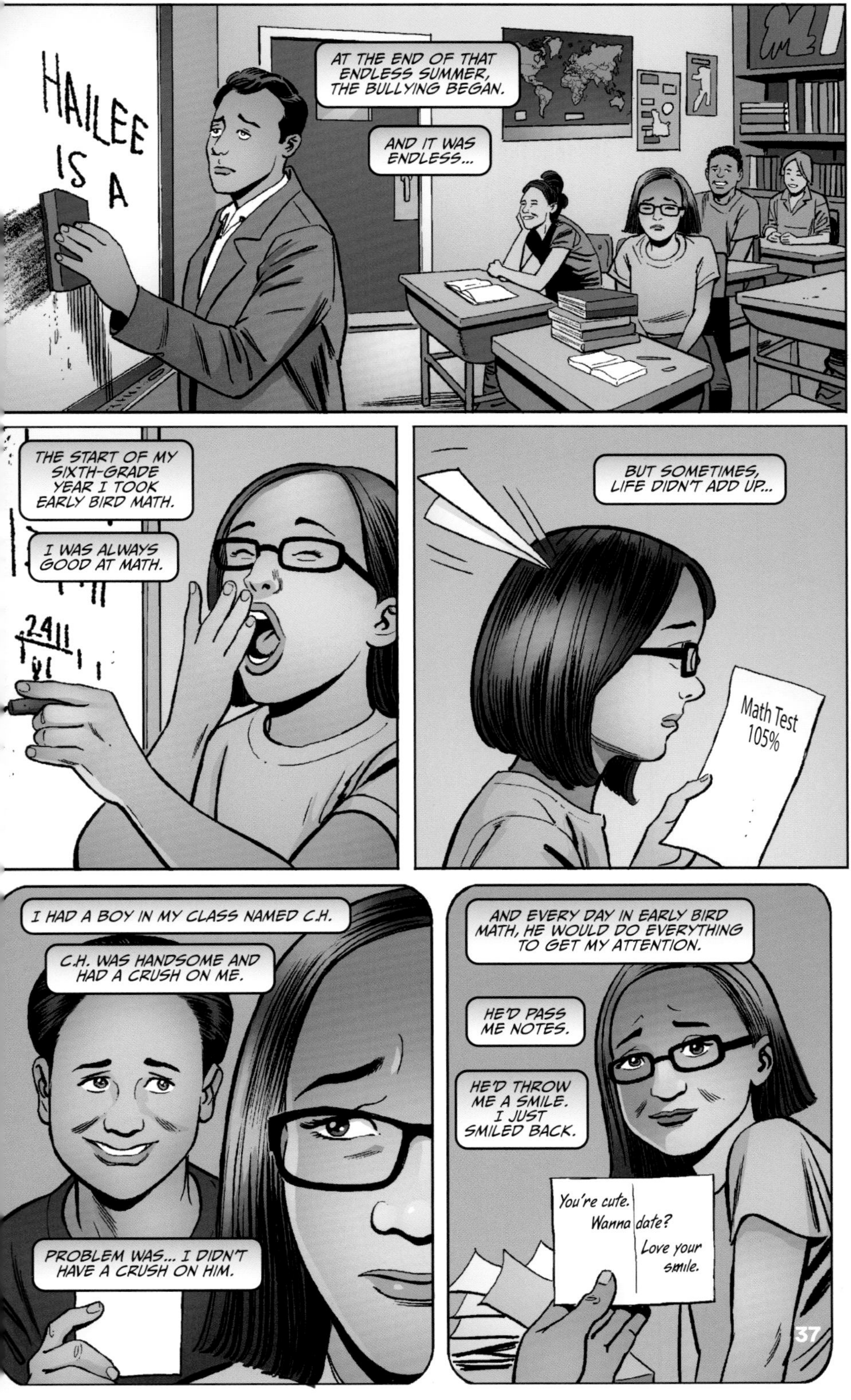
HAILEE IS A
AT THE END OF THAT ENDLESS SUMMER, THE BULLYING BEGAN.
AND IT WAS ENDLESS...
THE START OF MY SIXTH-GRADE YEAR I TOOK EARLY BIRD MATH.
I WAS ALWAYS GOOD AT MATH.
BUT SOMETIMES, LIFE DIDN'T ADD UP...
Math Test 105%
I HAD A BOY IN MY CLASS NAMED C.H.
C.H. WAS HANDSOME AND HAD A CRUSH ON ME.
PROBLEM WAS... I DIDN'T HAVE A CRUSH ON HIM.
AND EVERY DAY IN EARLY BIRD MATH, HE WOULD DO EVERYTHING TO GET MY ATTENTION.
HE'D PASS ME NOTES.
HE'D THROW ME A SMILE. I JUST SMILED BACK.
You're cute.
Wanna date?
Love your smile.

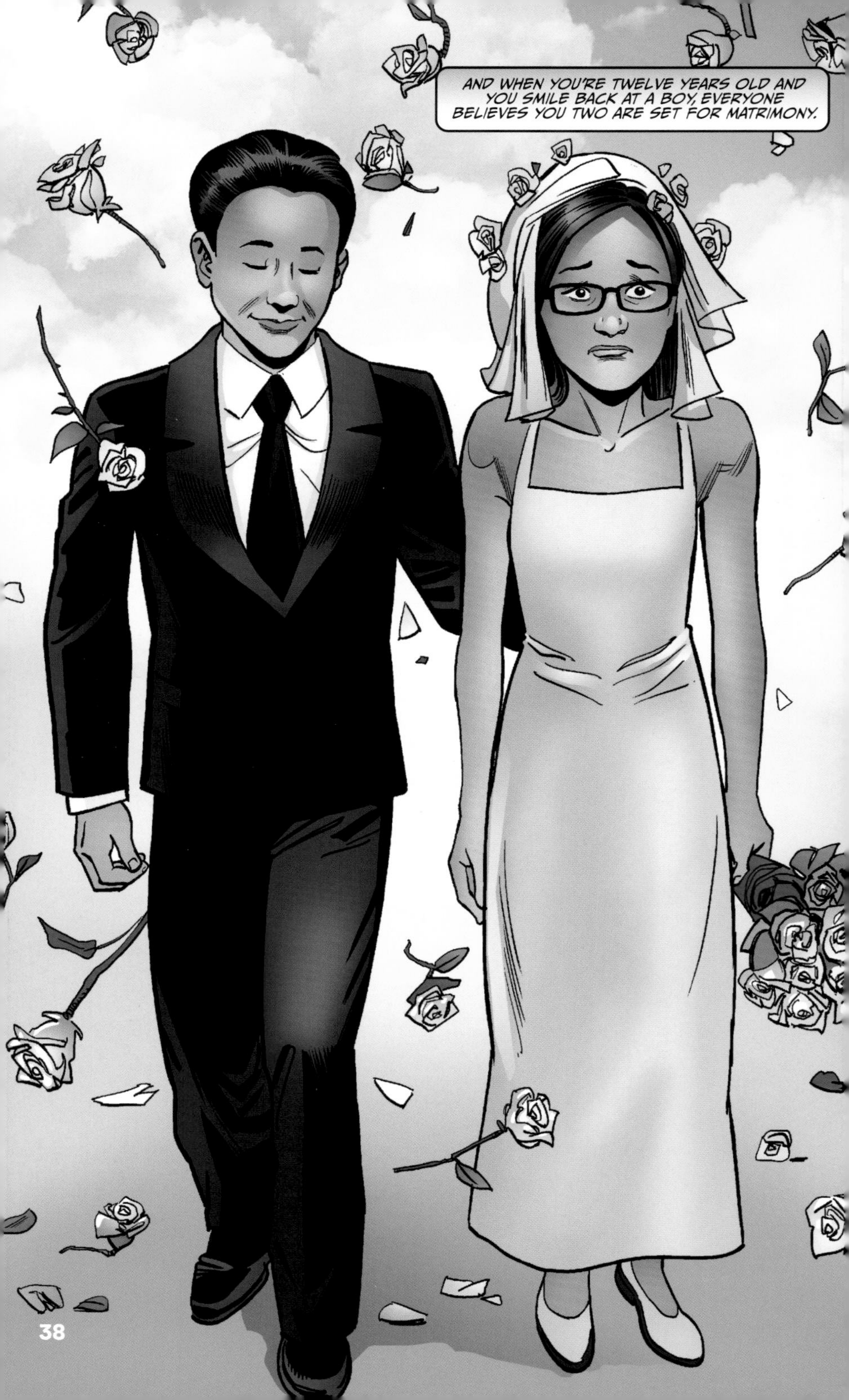
AND WHEN YOU'RE TWELVE YEARS OLD AND YOU SMILE BACK AT A BOY, EVERYONE BELIEVES YOU TWO ARE SET FOR MATRIMONY.

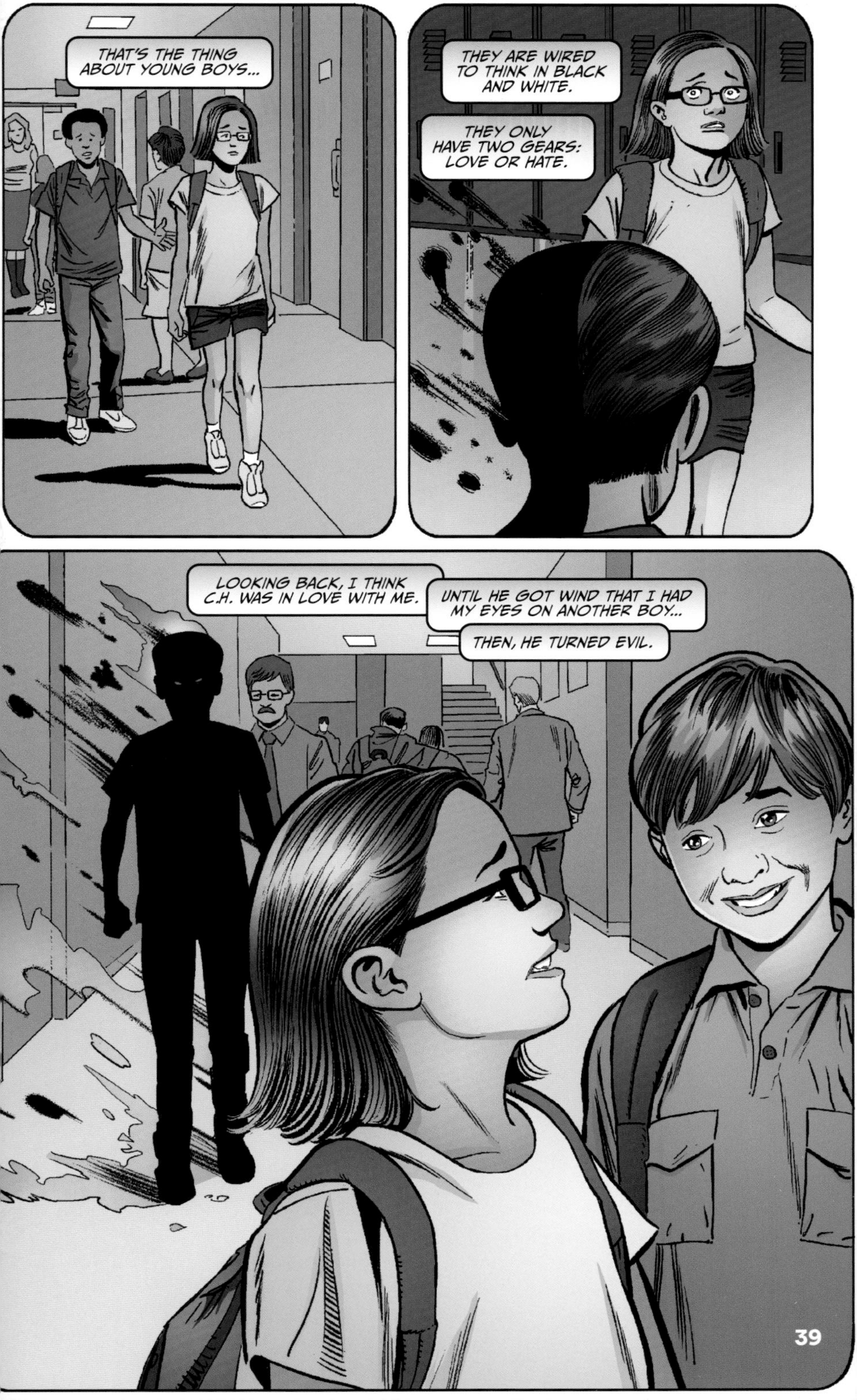
THAT'S THE THING ABOUT YOUNG BOYS...
THEY ARE WIRED TO THINK IN BLACK AND WHITE.
THEY ONLY HAVE TWO GEARS: LOVE OR HATE.
LOOKING BACK, I THINK C.H. WAS IN LOVE WITH ME.
UNTIL HE GOT WIND THAT I HAD MY EYES ON ANOTHER BOY...
THEN, HE TURNED EVIL.

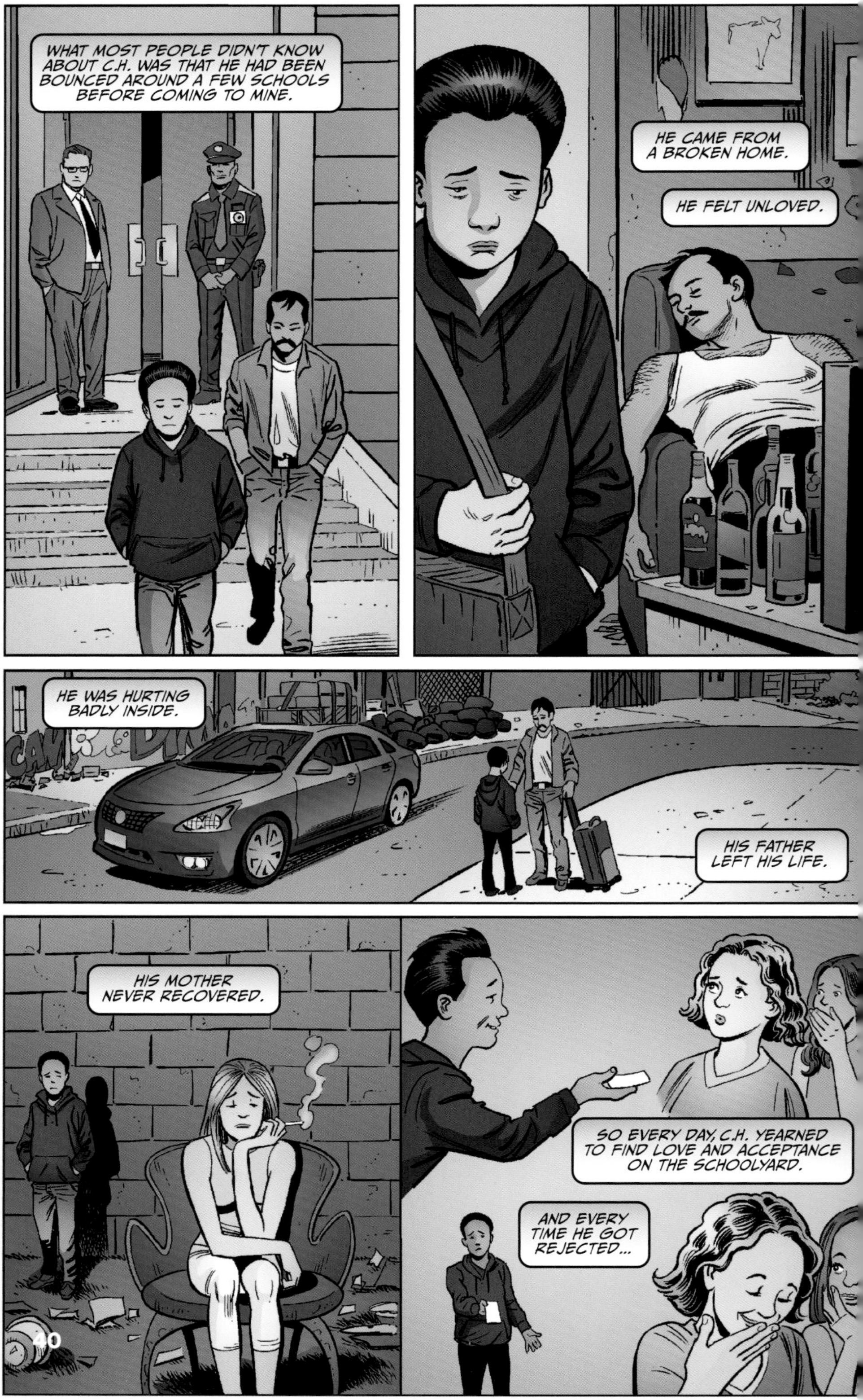
WHAT MOST PEOPLE DIDN'T KNOW ABOUT C.H. WAS THAT HE HAD BEEN BOUNCED AROUND A FEW SCHOOLS BEFORE COMING TO MINE.
HE CAME FROM A BROKEN HOME.
HE FELT UNLOVED.
HE WAS HURTING BADLY INSIDE.
HIS FATHER LEFT HIS LIFE.
HIS MOTHER NEVER RECOVERED.
SO EVERY DAY, C.H. YEARNED TO FIND LOVE AND ACCEPTANCE ON THE SCHOOLYARD.
AND EVERY TIME HE GOT REJECTED...

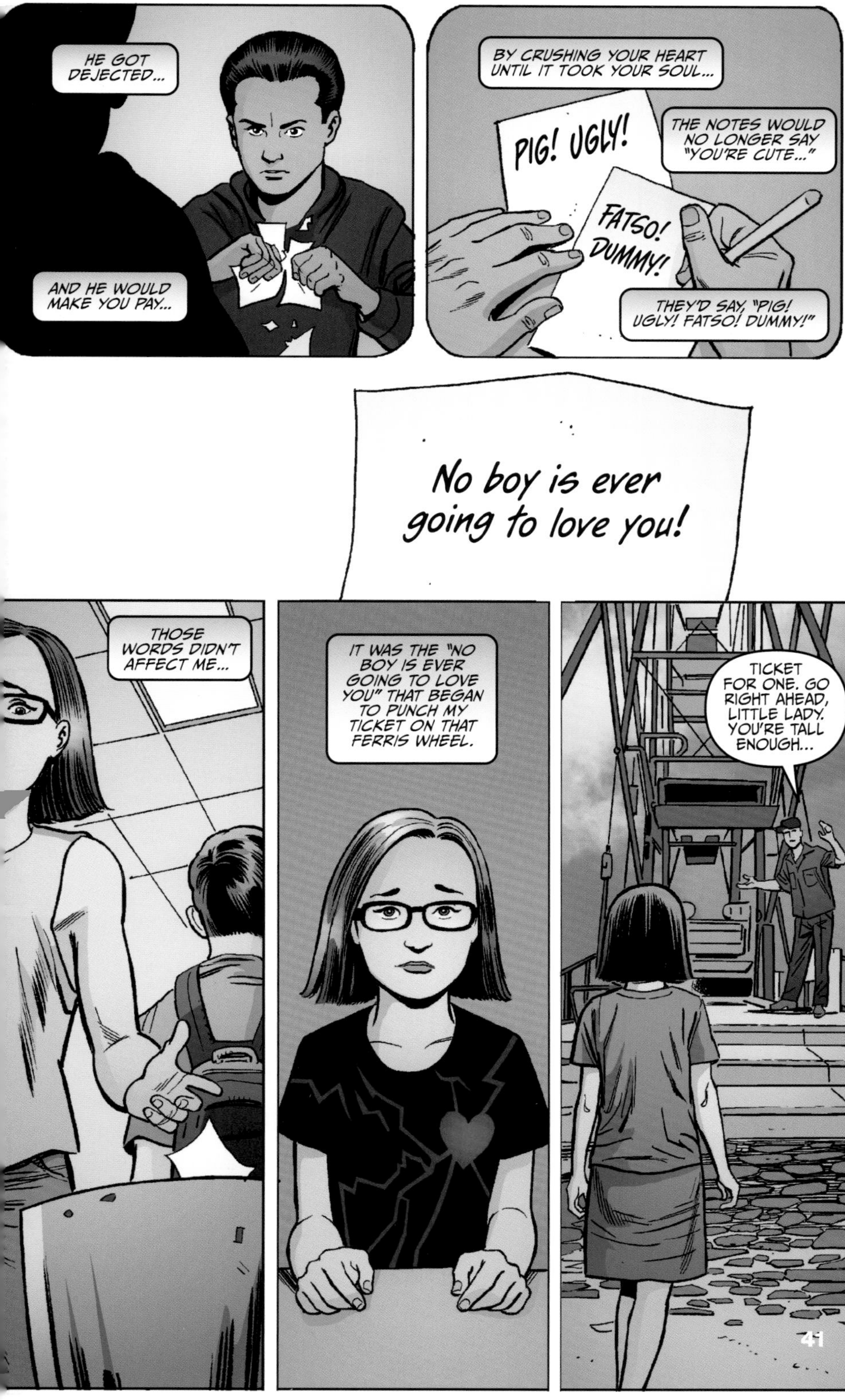
HE GOT DEJECTED...
AND HE WOULD MAKE YOU PAY...
BY CRUSHING YOUR HEART UNTIL IT TOOK YOUR SOUL...
PIG! UGLY!
THE NOTES WOULD NO LONGER SAY "YOU'RE CUTE..."
FATSO! DUMMY!
THEY'D SAY, "PIG! UGLY! FATSO! DUMMY!"
No boy is ever going to love you!
THOSE WORDS DIDN'T AFFECT ME...
IT WAS THE "NO BOY IS EVER GOING TO LOVE YOU" THAT BEGAN TO PUNCH MY TICKET ON THAT FERRIS WHEEL.
TICKET FOR ONE. GO RIGHT AHEAD, LITTLE LADY. YOU'RE TALL ENOUGH...

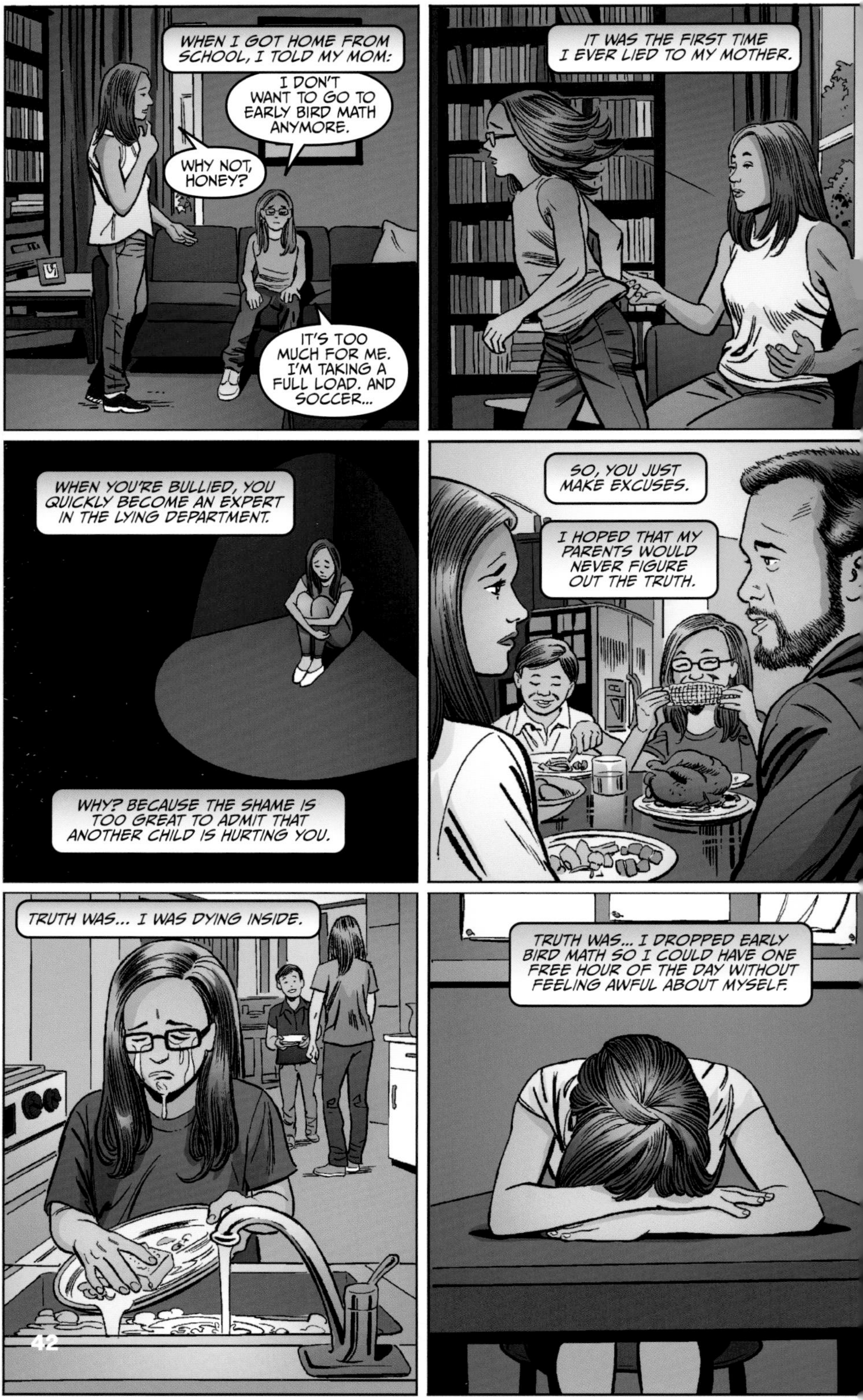

WHEN I GOT HOME FROM SCHOOL, I TOLD MY MOM:
I DON'T WANT TO GO TO EARLY BIRD MATH ANYMORE.
WHY NOT, HONEY?
IT'S TOO MUCH FOR ME. I'M TAKING A FULL LOAD. AND SOCCER...
IT WAS THE FIRST TIME I EVER LIED TO MY MOTHER.
WHEN YOU'RE BULLIED, YOU QUICKLY BECOME AN EXPERT IN THE LYING DEPARTMENT.
WHY? BECAUSE THE SHAME IS TOO GREAT TO ADMIT THAT ANOTHER CHILD IS HURTING YOU.
SO, YOU JUST MAKE EXCUSES.
I HOPED THAT MY PARENTS WOULD NEVER FIGURE OUT THE TRUTH.
TRUTH WAS... I WAS DYING INSIDE.
TRUTH WAS... I DROPPED EARLY BIRD MATH SO I COULD HAVE ONE FREE HOUR OF THE DAY WITHOUT FEELING AWFUL ABOUT MYSELF.

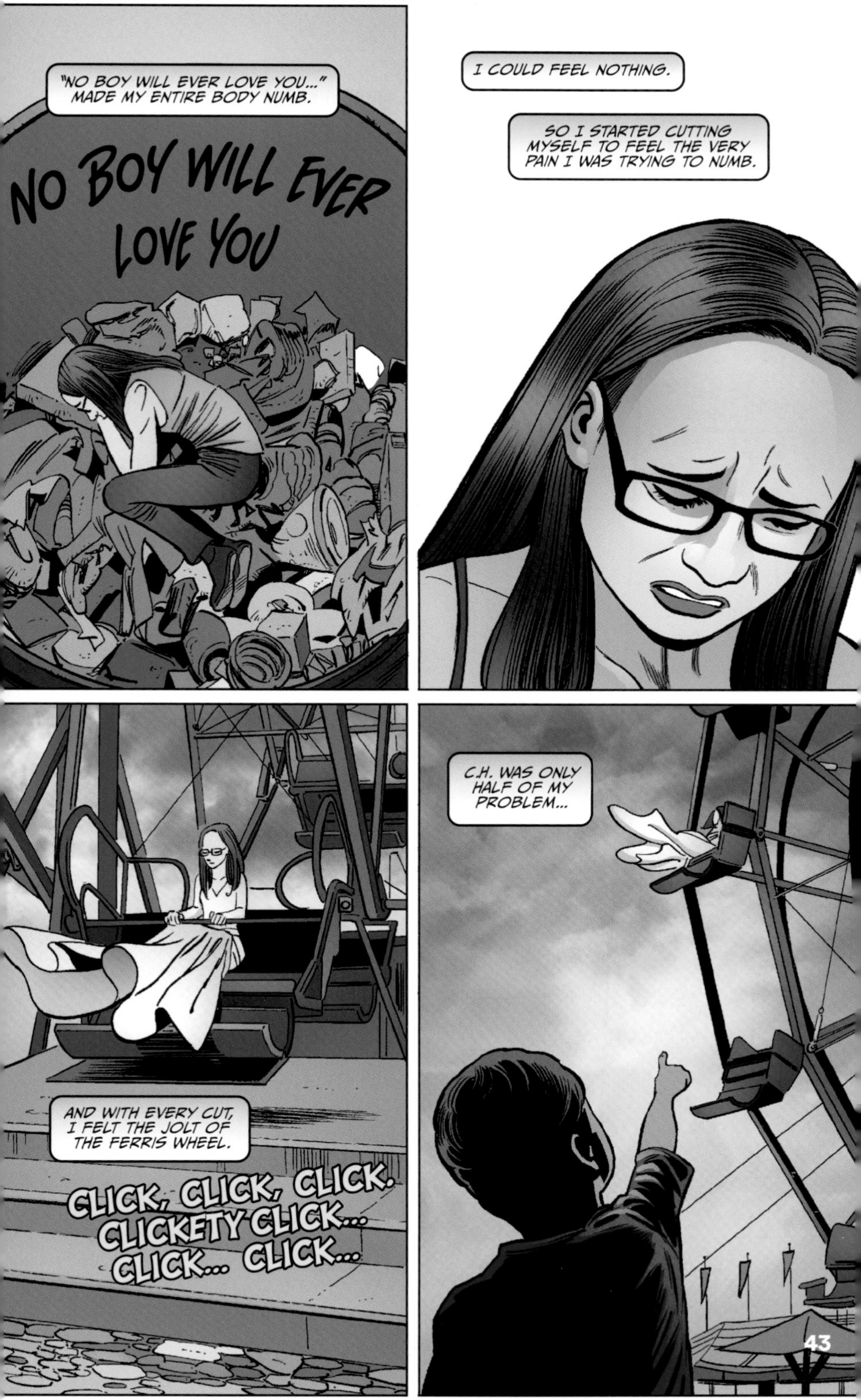
"NO BOY WILL EVER LOVE YOU..." MADE MY ENTIRE BODY NUMB.
NO BOY WILL EVER LOVE YOU
I COULD FEEL NOTHING.
SO I STARTED CUTTING MYSELF TO FEEL THE VERY PAIN I WAS TRYING TO NUMB.
AND WITH EVERY CUT, I FELT THE JOLT OF THE FERRIS WHEEL.
CLICK, CLICK, CLICK. CLICKETY CLICK... CLICK... CLICK...
C.H. WAS ONLY HALF OF MY PROBLEM...

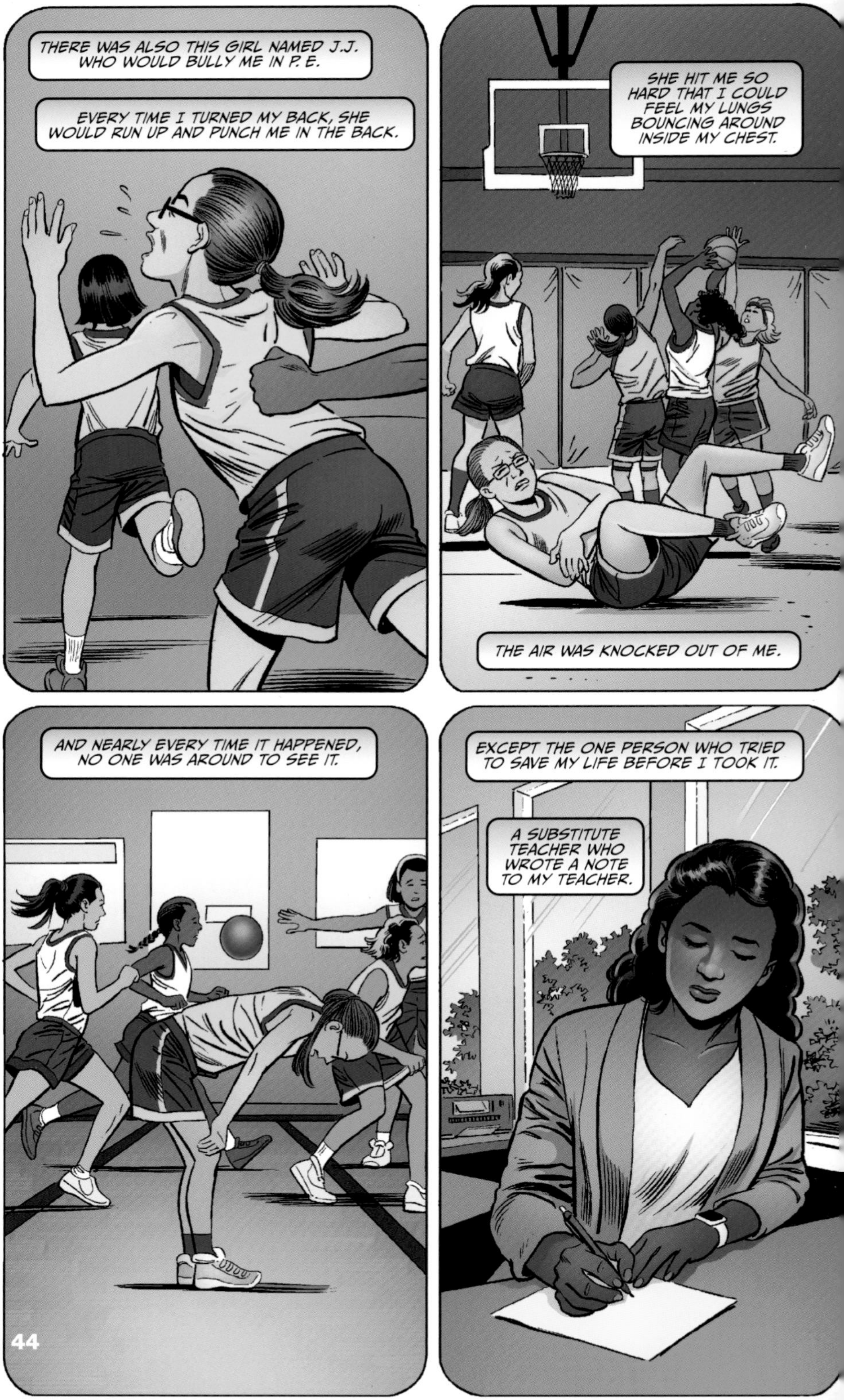
THERE WAS ALSO THIS GIRL NAMED J.J. WHO WOULD BULLY ME IN P. E.
EVERY TIME I TURNED MY BACK, SHE WOULD RUN UP AND PUNCH ME IN THE BACK.
SHE HIT ME SO HARD THAT I COULD FEEL MY LUNGS BOUNCING AROUND INSIDE MY CHEST.
THE AIR WAS KNOCKED OUT OF ME.
AND NEARLY EVERY TIME IT HAPPENED, NO ONE WAS AROUND TO SEE IT.
EXCEPT THE ONE PERSON WHO TRIED TO SAVE MY LIFE BEFORE I TOOK IT.
A SUBSTITUTE TEACHER WHO WROTE A NOTE TO MY TEACHER.

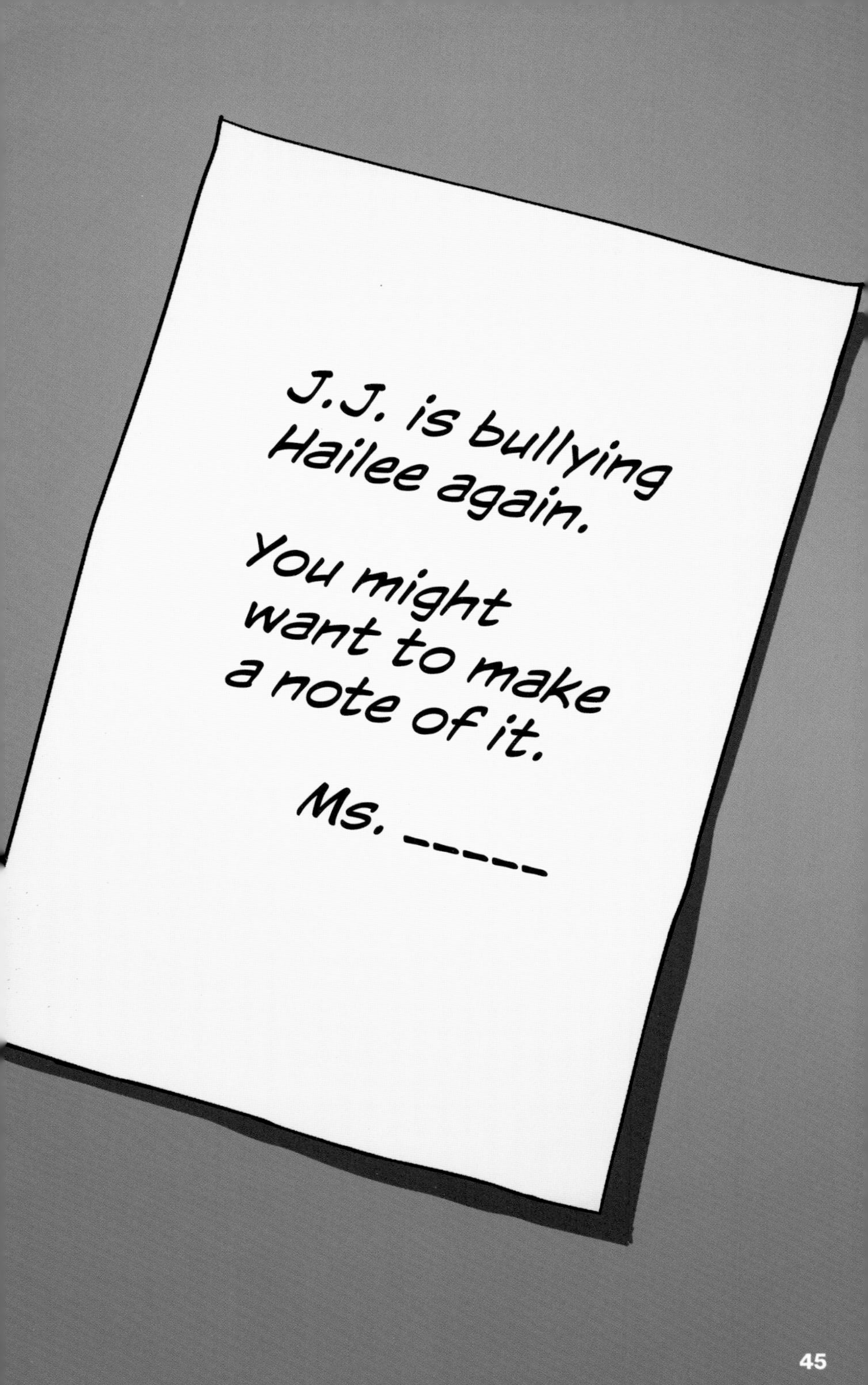
J.J. is bullying Hailee again.
You might want to make a note of it.
Ms. ______

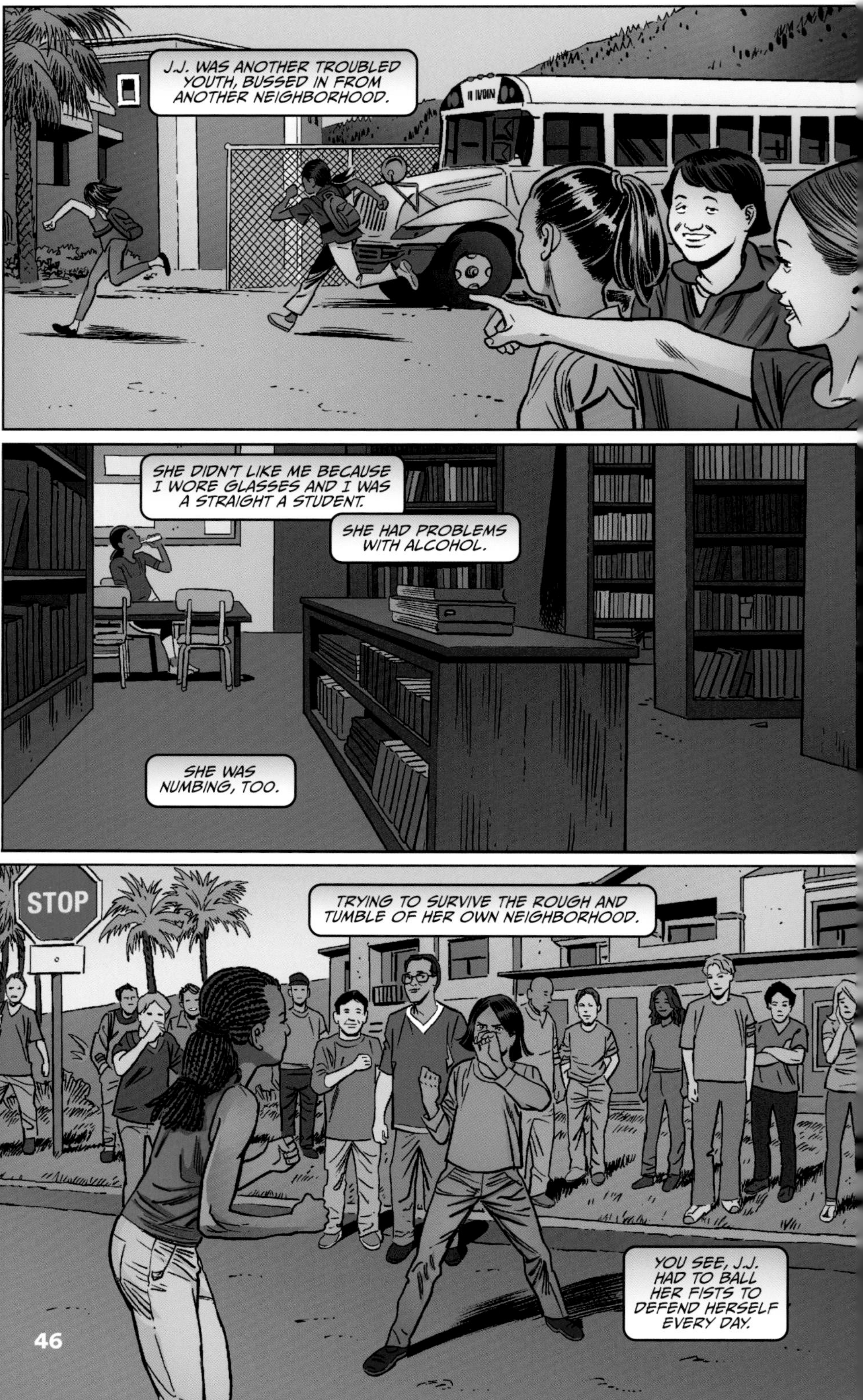
J.J. WAS ANOTHER TROUBLED YOUTH, BUSSED IN FROM ANOTHER NEIGHBORHOOD.
SHE DIDN'T LIKE ME BECAUSE I WORE GLASSES AND I WAS A STRAIGHT A STUDENT.
SHE HAD PROBLEMS WITH ALCOHOL.
SHE WAS NUMBING, TOO.
STOP
TRYING TO SURVIVE THE ROUGH AND TUMBLE OF HER OWN NEIGHBORHOOD.
YOU SEE, J.J. HAD TO BALL HER FISTS TO DEFEND HERSELF EVERY DAY.

SHE HAD TO FIGHT NEIGHBORHOOD KIDS FOR THE RIGHT TO GET OUT.

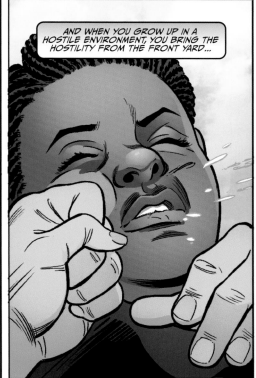

AND WHEN YOU GROW UP IN A HOSTILE ENVIRONMENT, YOU BRING THE HOSTILITY FROM THE FRONT YARD...

...TO THE SCHOOLYARD.

AND THIS IS WHERE THE VICIOUS CYCLE OF BULLYING BEGINS...

47

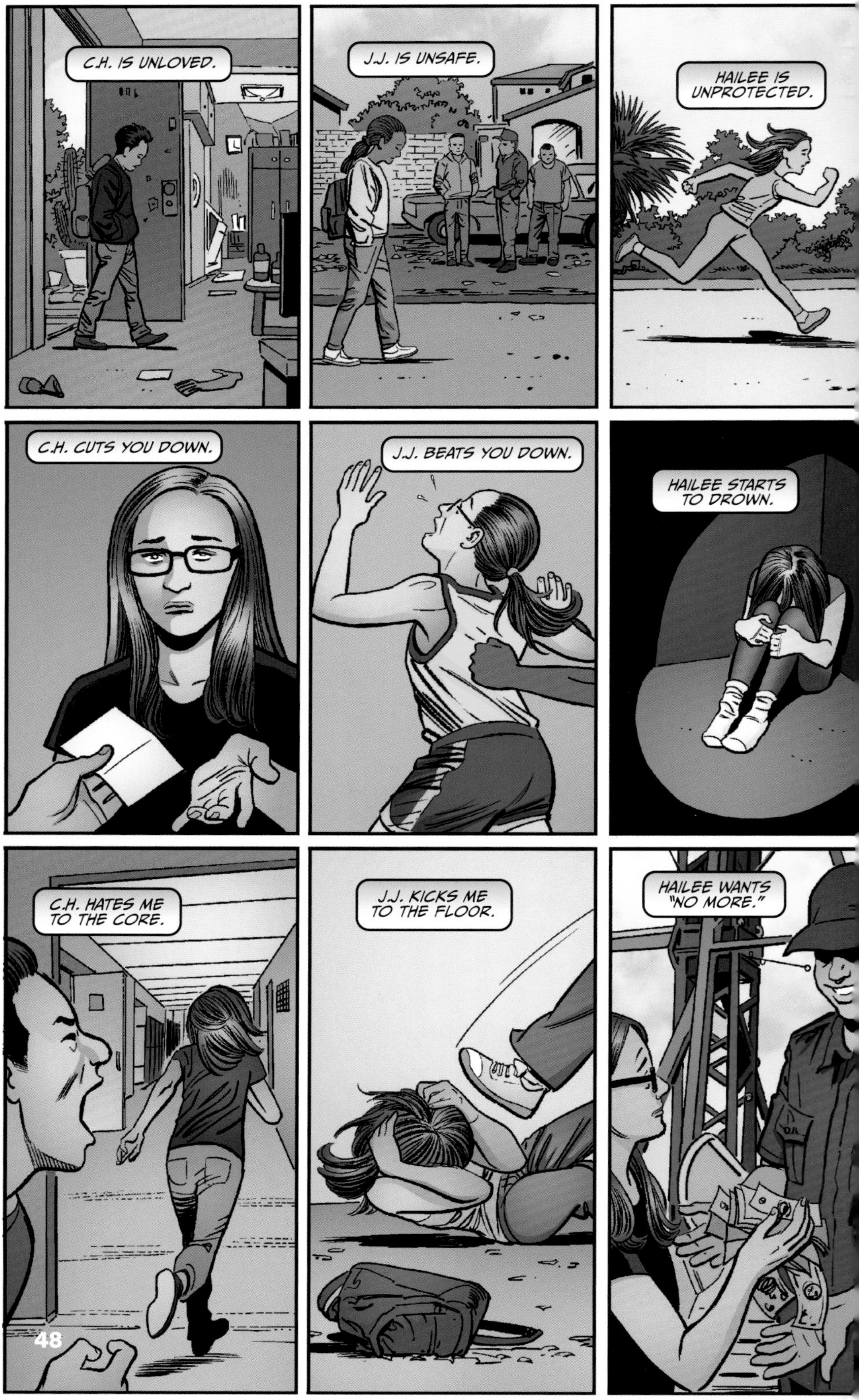
C.H. IS UNLOVED.
J.J. IS UNSAFE.
HAILEE IS UNPROTECTED.
C.H. CUTS YOU DOWN.
J.J. BEATS YOU DOWN.
HAILEE STARTS TO DROWN.
C.H. HATES ME TO THE CORE.
J.J. KICKS ME TO THE FLOOR.
HAILEE WANTS "NO MORE."

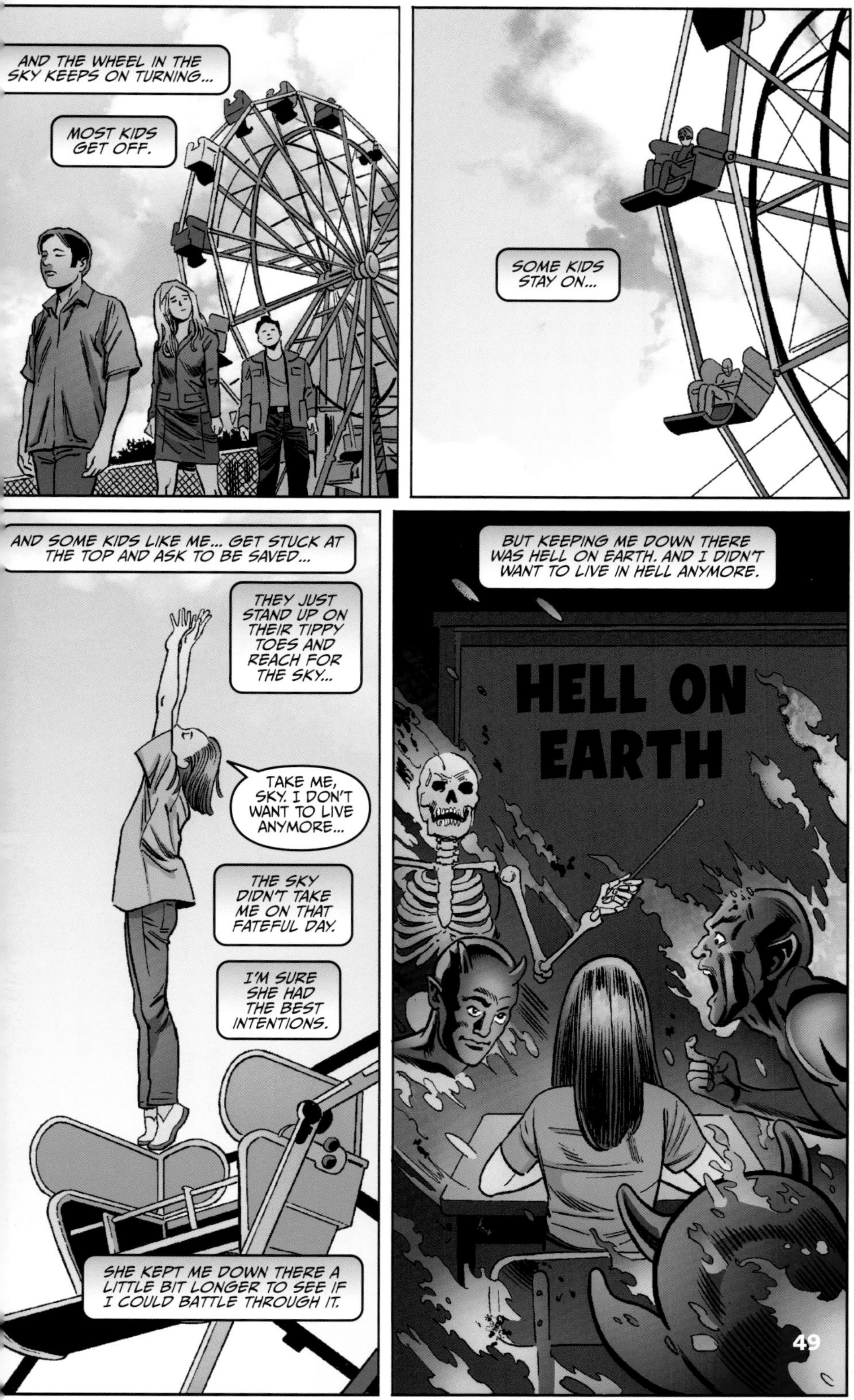
AND THE WHEEL IN THE SKY KEEPS ON TURNING...
MOST KIDS GET OFF.
SOME KIDS STAY ON...
AND SOME KIDS LIKE ME... GET STUCK AT THE TOP AND ASK TO BE SAVED...
THEY JUST STAND UP ON THEIR TIPPY TOES AND REACH FOR THE SKY...
TAKE ME, SKY. I DON'T WANT TO LIVE ANYMORE...
THE SKY DIDN'T TAKE ME ON THAT FATEFUL DAY.
I'M SURE SHE HAD THE BEST INTENTIONS.
SHE KEPT ME DOWN THERE A LITTLE BIT LONGER TO SEE IF I COULD BATTLE THROUGH IT.
BUT KEEPING ME DOWN THERE WAS HELL ON EARTH. AND I DIDN'T WANT TO LIVE IN HELL ANYMORE.
HELL ON EARTH

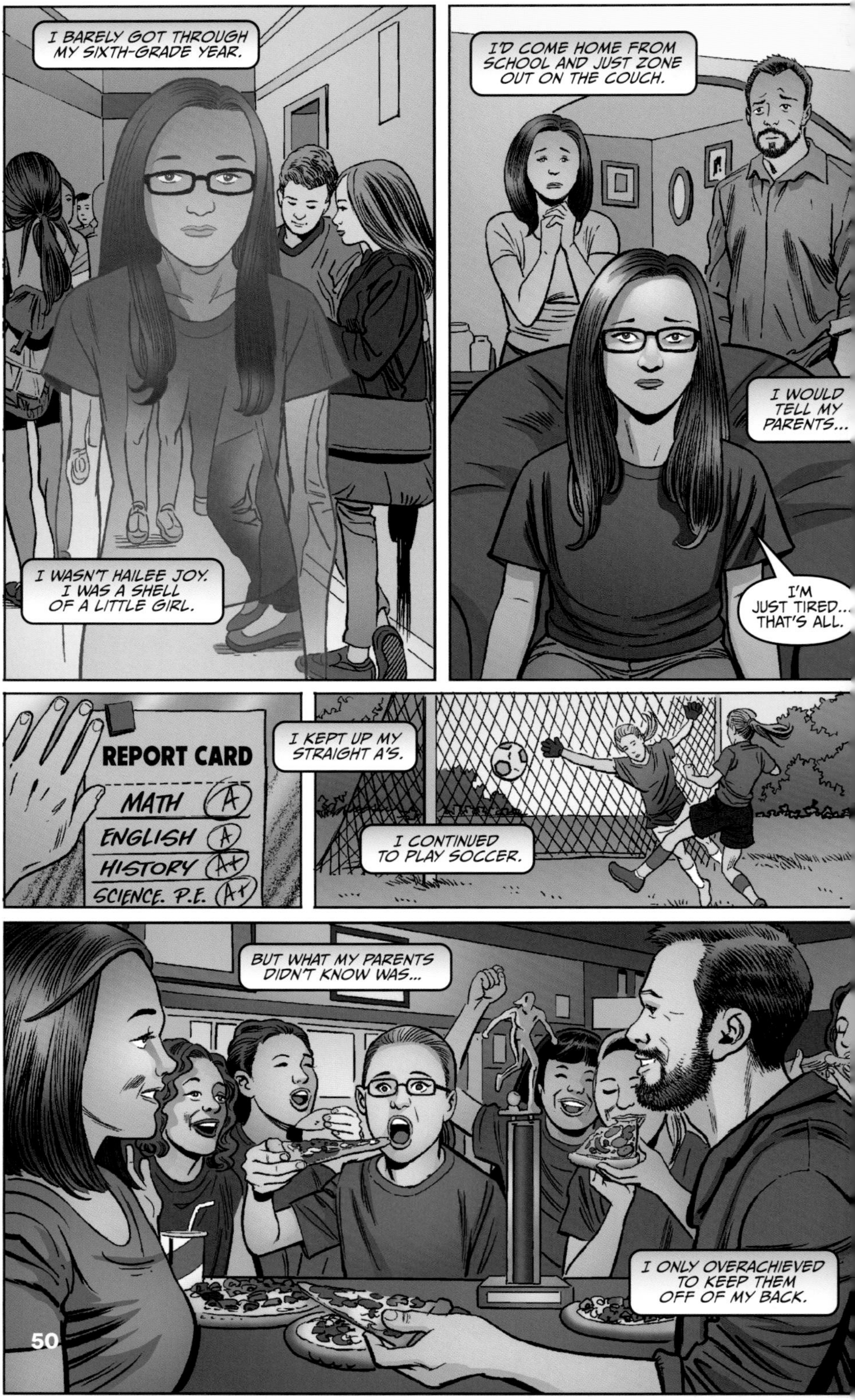
I BARELY GOT THROUGH MY SIXTH-GRADE YEAR.
I WASN'T HAILEE JOY. I WAS A SHELL OF A LITTLE GIRL.
I'D COME HOME FROM SCHOOL AND JUST ZONE OUT ON THE COUCH.
I WOULD TELL MY PARENTS...
I'M JUST TIRED... THAT'S ALL.
REPORT CARD
MATH A
ENGLISH A
HISTORY A+
SCIENCE. P.E. A+
I KEPT UP MY STRAIGHT A'S.
I CONTINUED TO PLAY SOCCER.
BUT WHAT MY PARENTS DIDN'T KNOW WAS...
I ONLY OVERACHIEVED TO KEEP THEM OFF OF MY BACK.

I DIDN'T WANT THEM TO FIND OUT ABOUT ANY OF THE BULLYING.

THE LAST THING I NEEDED WAS MY PARENTS RAISING A STINK AND MAKING IT WORSE.

OU OKAY? OU'VE BEEN N THERE A ONG TIME.

I'M FINE, MOM. JUST COMBING MY HAIR...

SO, I CUT TIES WITH REALITY...

AS I CUT FLESH WITH MY PAIN...

...

I DIDN'T KNOW WHERE ELSE TO TURN...

MY LIFE WAS A TICKING CLOCK.

THE CIRCULAR CYCLES OF LIFE WERE BECOMING INDISTINGUISHABLE.

ONE COUNTED TIME...

THE OTHER COUNTED MY TIME...

51

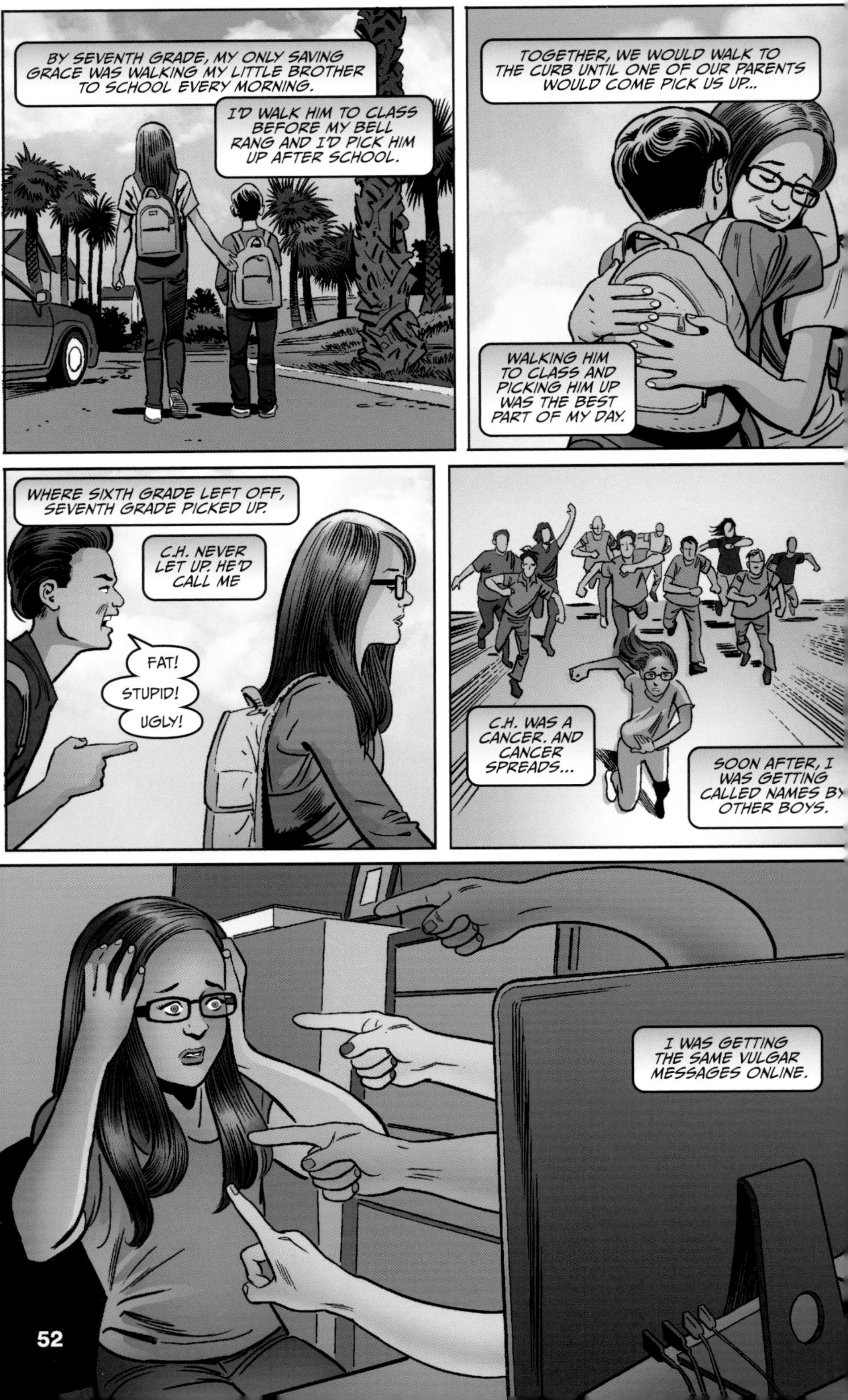
BY SEVENTH GRADE, MY ONLY SAVING GRACE WAS WALKING MY LITTLE BROTHER TO SCHOOL EVERY MORNING.
I'D WALK HIM TO CLASS BEFORE MY BELL RANG AND I'D PICK HIM UP AFTER SCHOOL.
TOGETHER, WE WOULD WALK TO THE CURB UNTIL ONE OF OUR PARENTS WOULD COME PICK US UP...
WALKING HIM TO CLASS AND PICKING HIM UP WAS THE BEST PART OF MY DAY.
WHERE SIXTH GRADE LEFT OFF, SEVENTH GRADE PICKED UP.
C.H. NEVER LET UP. HE'D CALL ME
FAT!
STUPID!
UGLY!
C.H. WAS A CANCER. AND CANCER SPREADS...
SOON AFTER, I WAS GETTING CALLED NAMES BY OTHER BOYS.
I WAS GETTING THE SAME VULGAR MESSAGES ONLINE.

I JUST COULDN'T ESCAPE IT.

FAT WORTHLESS UGLY FAT WORTHLESS UGLY FAT WORTH FAT FAT WORTHLESS UGLY FAT WORTHLESS

INSTEAD OF GETTING PUNCHED IN THE BACK, I WAS GETTING STABBED IN THE HEART.

AND CARRYING THAT SECRET AROUND WHEN I GOT BACK HOME WAS THE TOUGHEST OF ALL.

I HAD TO PUT ON THE MOST DIFFICULT FACE AROUND MY PARENTS.

THE FACE OF "NORMAL."

THE IMPOSSIBLE BURDEN OF COMING OFF HAPPY WHEN I WAS INSURMOUNTABLY SAD.

SO, I DID WHATEVER I COULD TO MAKE IT THROUGH THE DAY.

I PUT TOGETHER A SCRAP BOOK OF ALL OF MY FONDEST MEMORIES AND CARRIED IT IN MY BACKPACK.

PICTURES OF ME AND MY BROTHER.

53

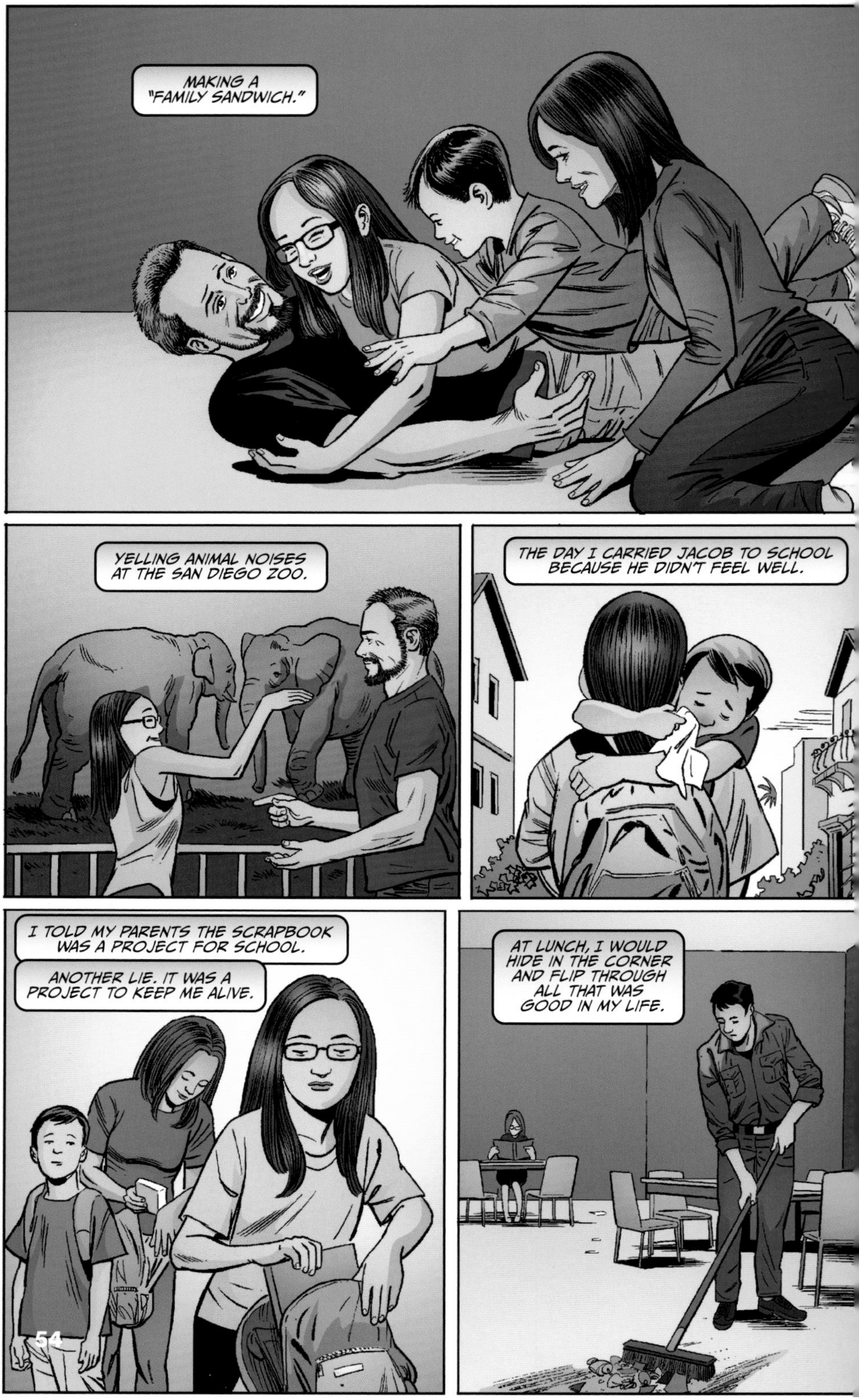
MAKING A "FAMILY SANDWICH."
YELLING ANIMAL NOISES AT THE SAN DIEGO ZOO.
THE DAY I CARRIED JACOB TO SCHOOL BECAUSE HE DIDN'T FEEL WELL.
I TOLD MY PARENTS THE SCRAPBOOK WAS A PROJECT FOR SCHOOL.
ANOTHER LIE. IT WAS A PROJECT TO KEEP ME ALIVE.
AT LUNCH, I WOULD HIDE IN THE CORNER AND FLIP THROUGH ALL THAT WAS GOOD IN MY LIFE.

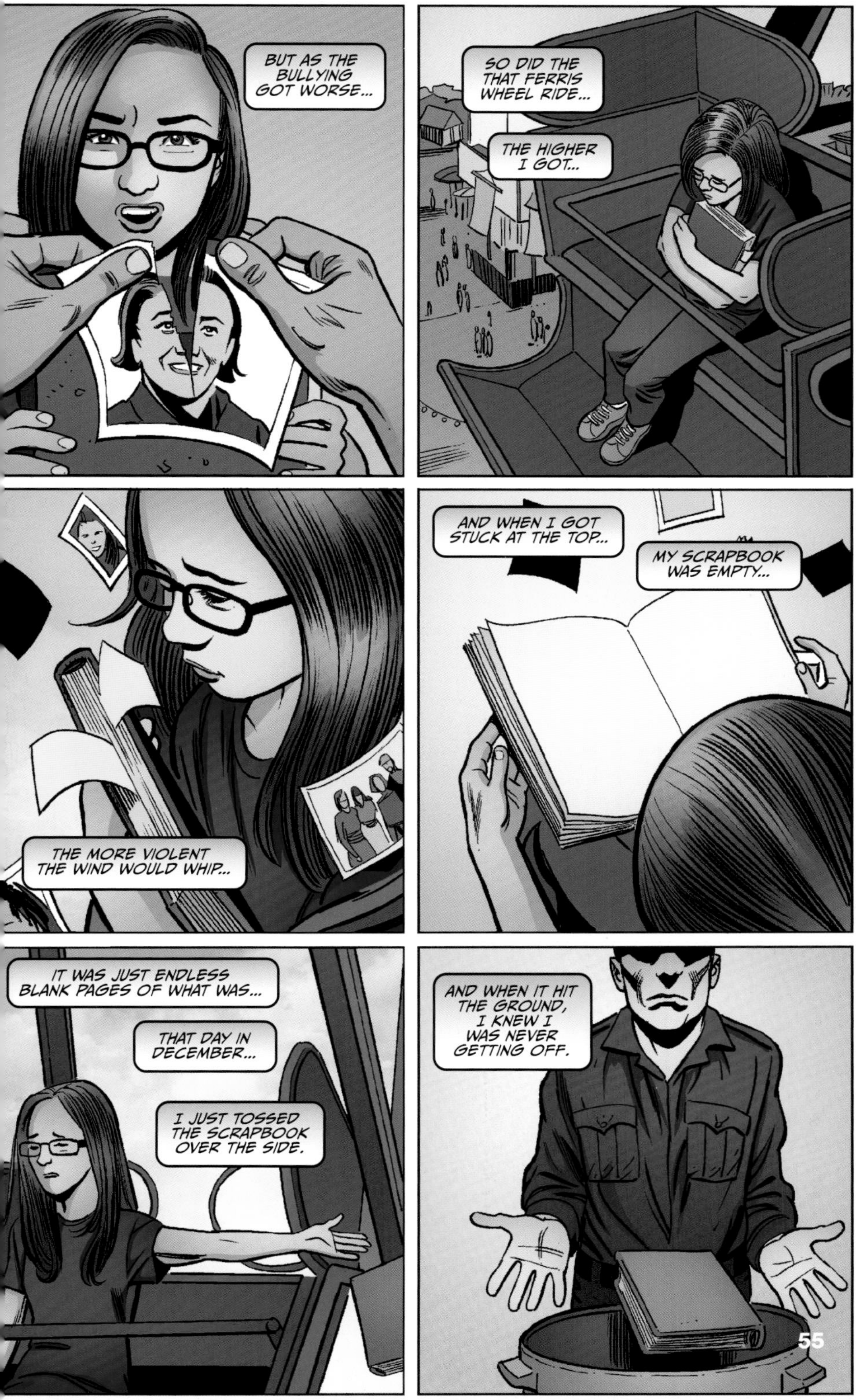
BUT AS THE BULLYING GOT WORSE...
SO DID THE THAT FERRIS WHEEL RIDE...
THE HIGHER I GOT...
THE MORE VIOLENT THE WIND WOULD WHIP...
AND WHEN I GOT STUCK AT THE TOP...
MY SCRAPBOOK WAS EMPTY...
IT WAS JUST ENDLESS BLANK PAGES OF WHAT WAS...
THAT DAY IN DECEMBER...
I JUST TOSSED THE SCRAPBOOK OVER THE SIDE.
AND WHEN IT HIT THE GROUND, I KNEW I WAS NEVER GETTING OFF.

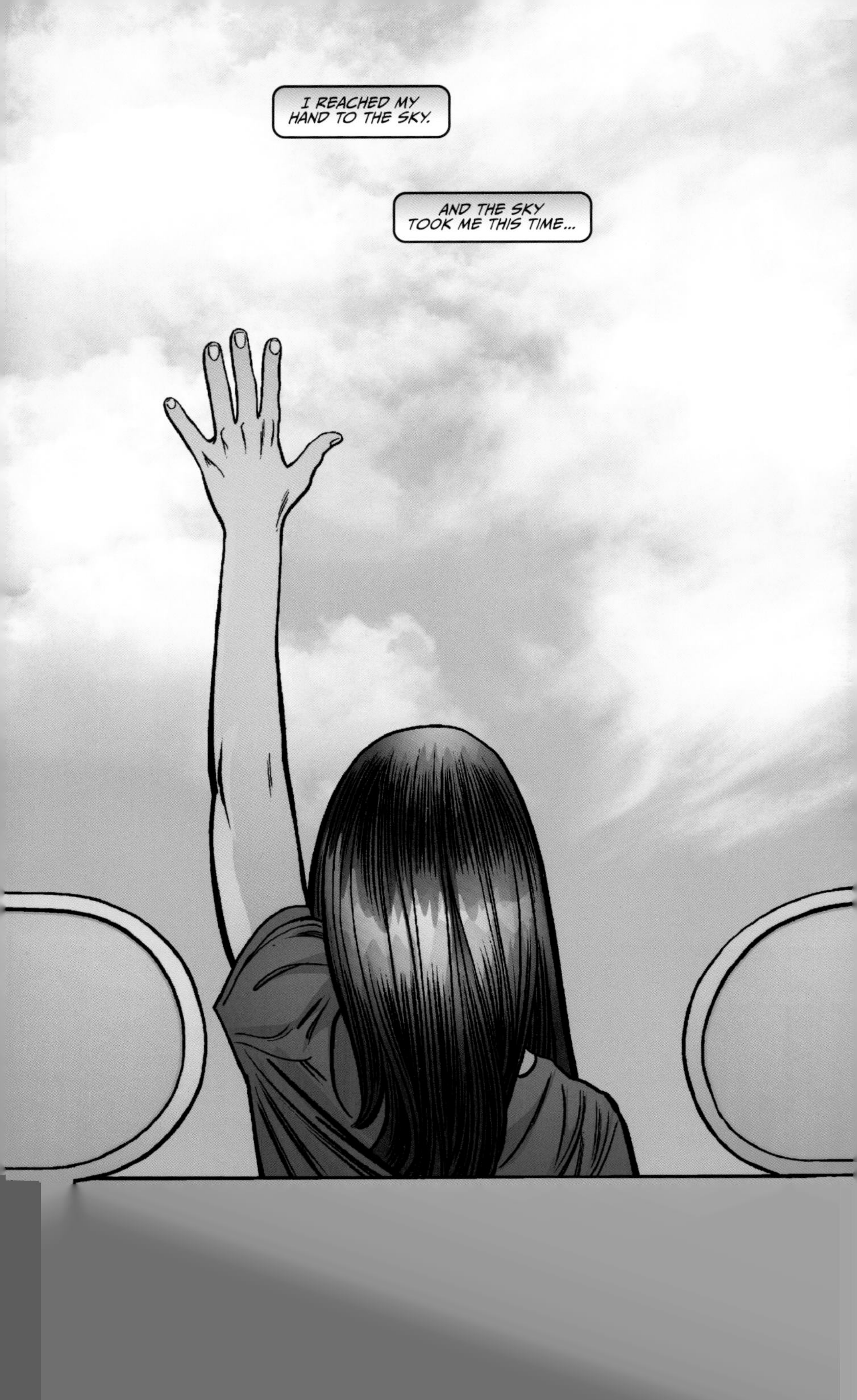
I REACHED MY HAND TO THE SKY.
AND THE SKY TOOK ME THIS TIME...

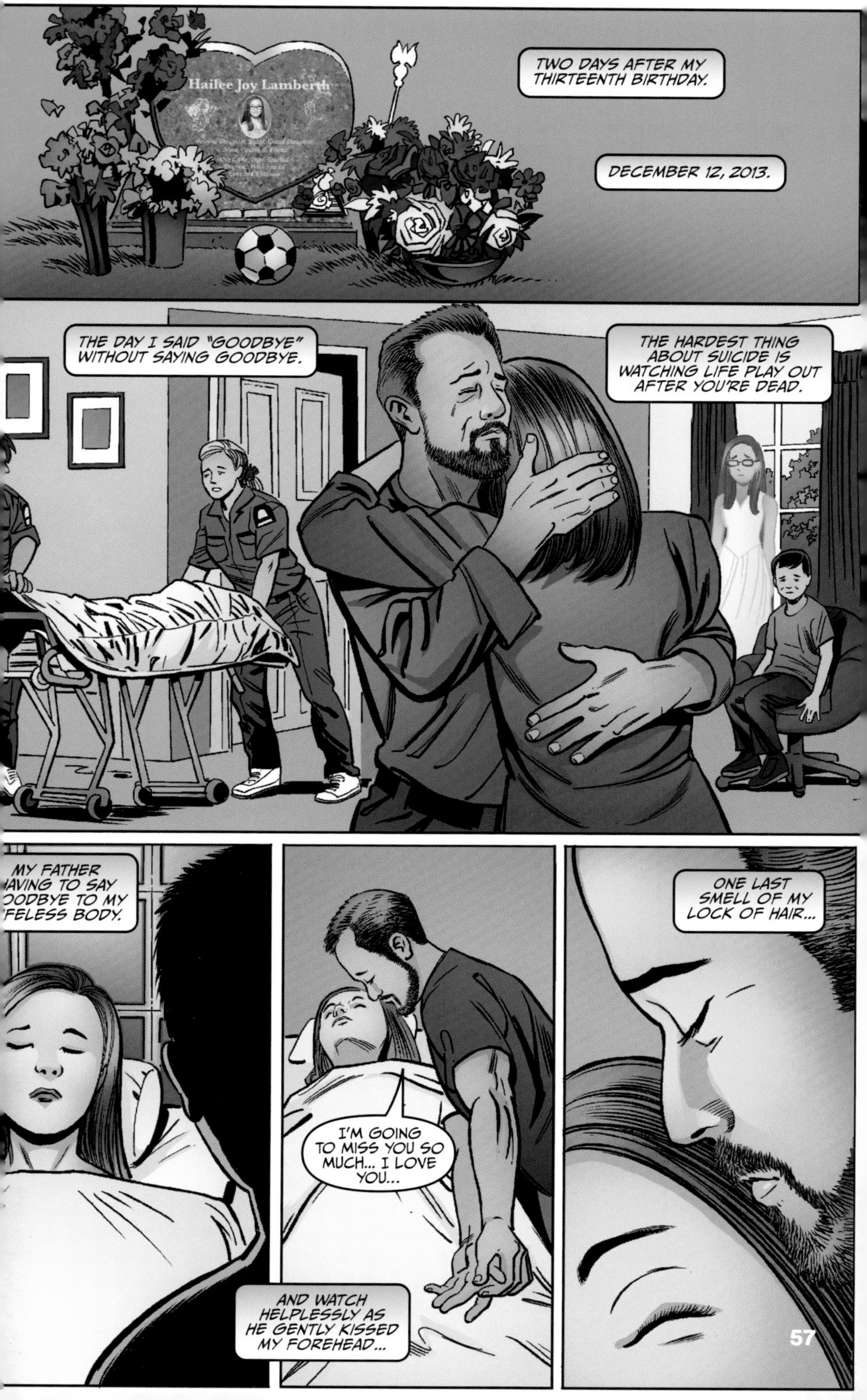
Hailee Joy Lamberth
TWO DAYS AFTER MY THIRTEENTH BIRTHDAY.
DECEMBER 12, 2013.
THE DAY I SAID "GOODBYE" WITHOUT SAYING GOODBYE.
THE HARDEST THING ABOUT SUICIDE IS WATCHING LIFE PLAY OUT AFTER YOU'RE DEAD.
MY FATHER
IAVING TO SAY
OODBYE TO MY
FELESS BODY.
I'M GOING TO MISS YOU SO MUCH... I LOVE YOU...
AND WATCH HELPLESSLY AS HE GENTLY KISSED MY FOREHEAD...
ONE LAST SMELL OF MY LOCK OF HAIR...

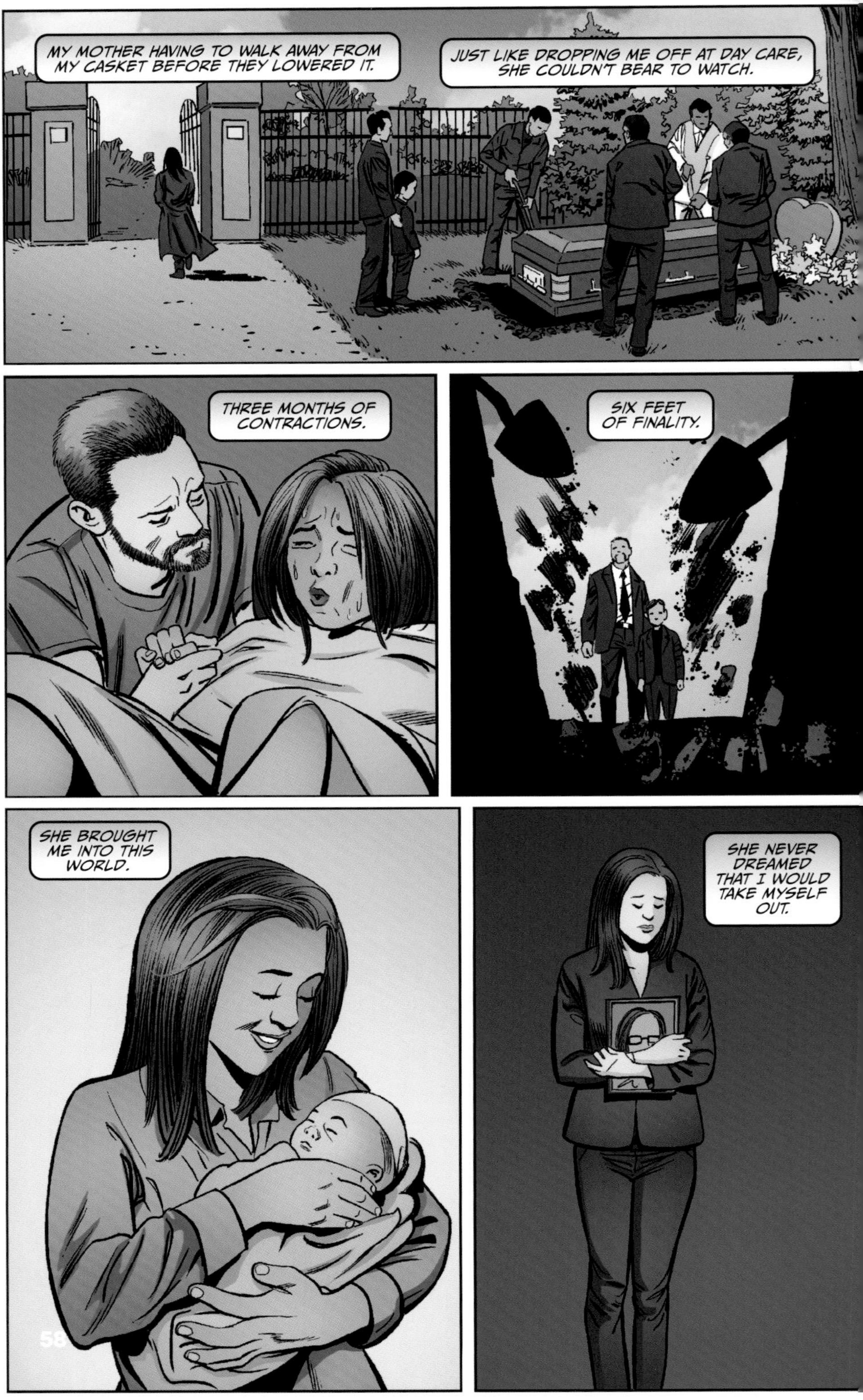

MY MOTHER HAVING TO WALK AWAY FROM MY CASKET BEFORE THEY LOWERED IT.
JUST LIKE DROPPING ME OFF AT DAY CARE, SHE COULDN'T BEAR TO WATCH.
THREE MONTHS OF CONTRACTIONS.
SIX FEET OF FINALITY.
SHE BROUGHT ME INTO THIS WORLD.
SHE NEVER DREAMED THAT I WOULD TAKE MYSELF OUT.

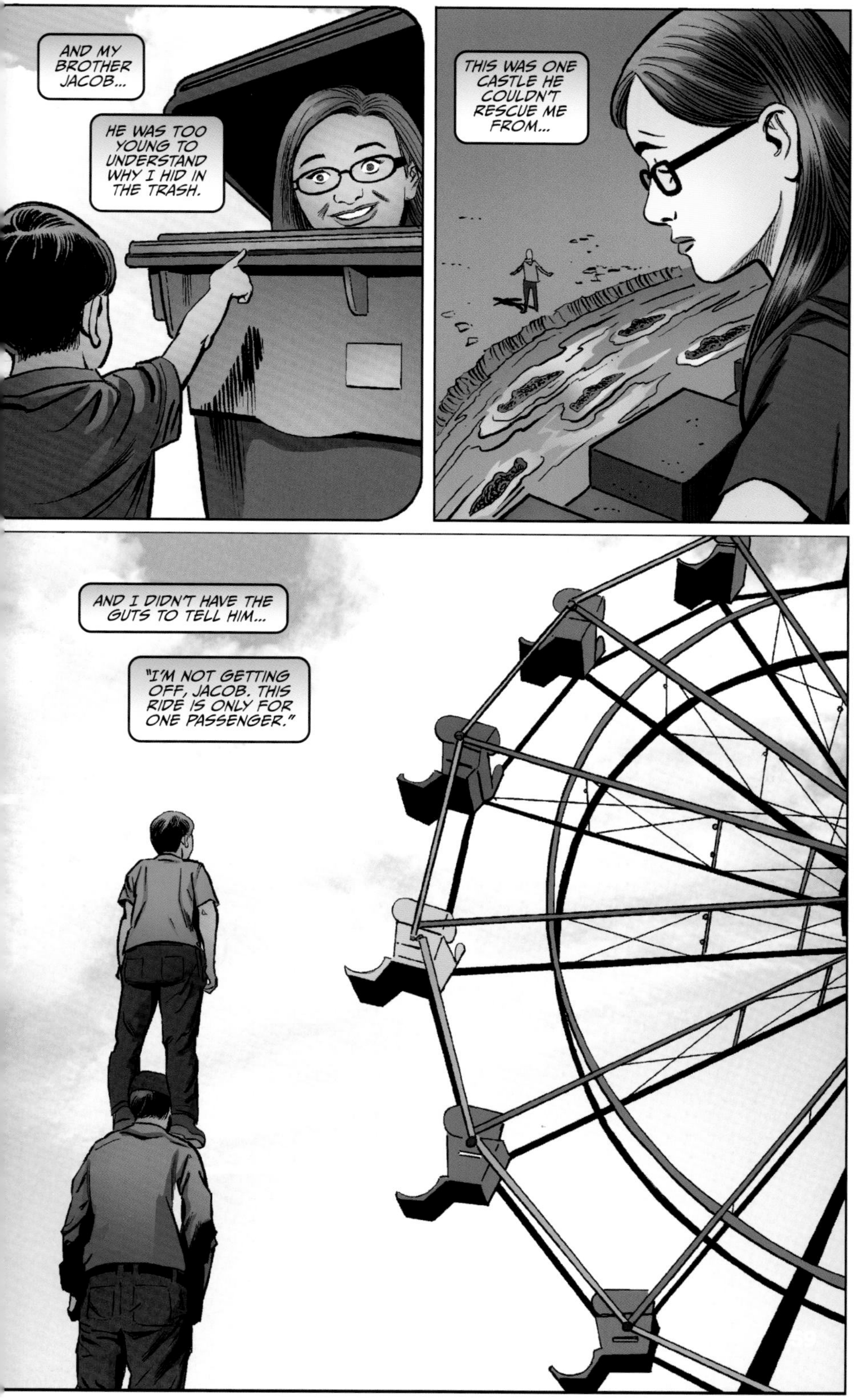
AND MY BROTHER JACOB...
HE WAS TOO YOUNG TO UNDERSTAND WHY I HID IN THE TRASH.
THIS WAS ONE CASTLE HE COULDN'T RESCUE ME FROM...
AND I DIDN'T HAVE THE GUTS TO TELL HIM...
"I'M NOT GETTING OFF, JACOB. THIS RIDE IS ONLY FOR ONE PASSENGER."

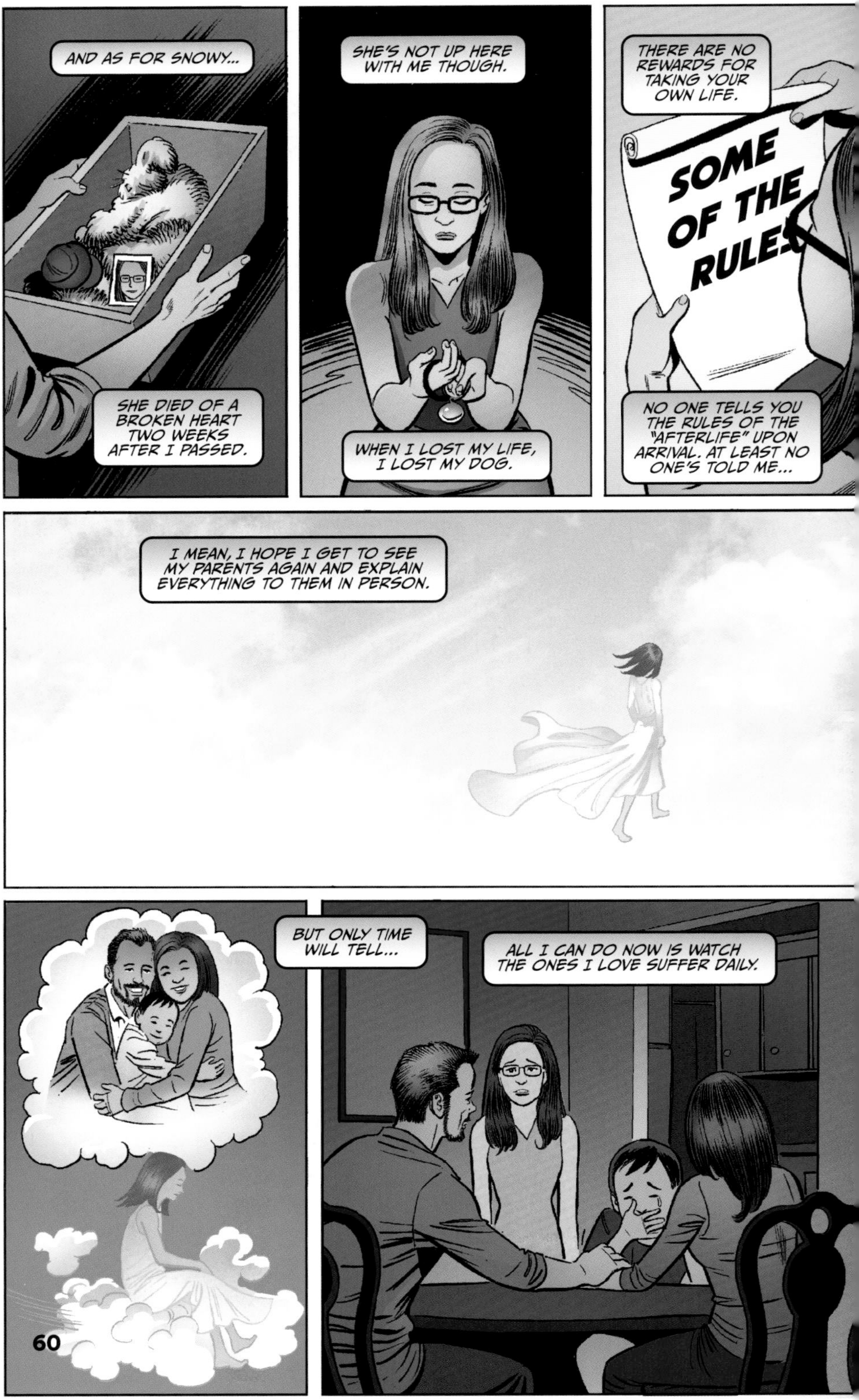
AND AS FOR SNOWY...
SHE DIED OF A BROKEN HEART TWO WEEKS AFTER I PASSED.
SHE'S NOT UP HERE WITH ME THOUGH.
WHEN I LOST MY LIFE, I LOST MY DOG.
THERE ARE NO REWARDS FOR TAKING YOUR OWN LIFE.
SOME OF THE RULES
NO ONE TELLS YOU THE RULES OF THE "AFTERLIFE" UPON ARRIVAL. AT LEAST NO ONE'S TOLD ME...
I MEAN, I HOPE I GET TO SEE MY PARENTS AGAIN AND EXPLAIN EVERYTHING TO THEM IN PERSON.
BUT ONLY TIME WILL TELL...
ALL I CAN DO NOW IS WATCH THE ONES I LOVE SUFFER DAILY.

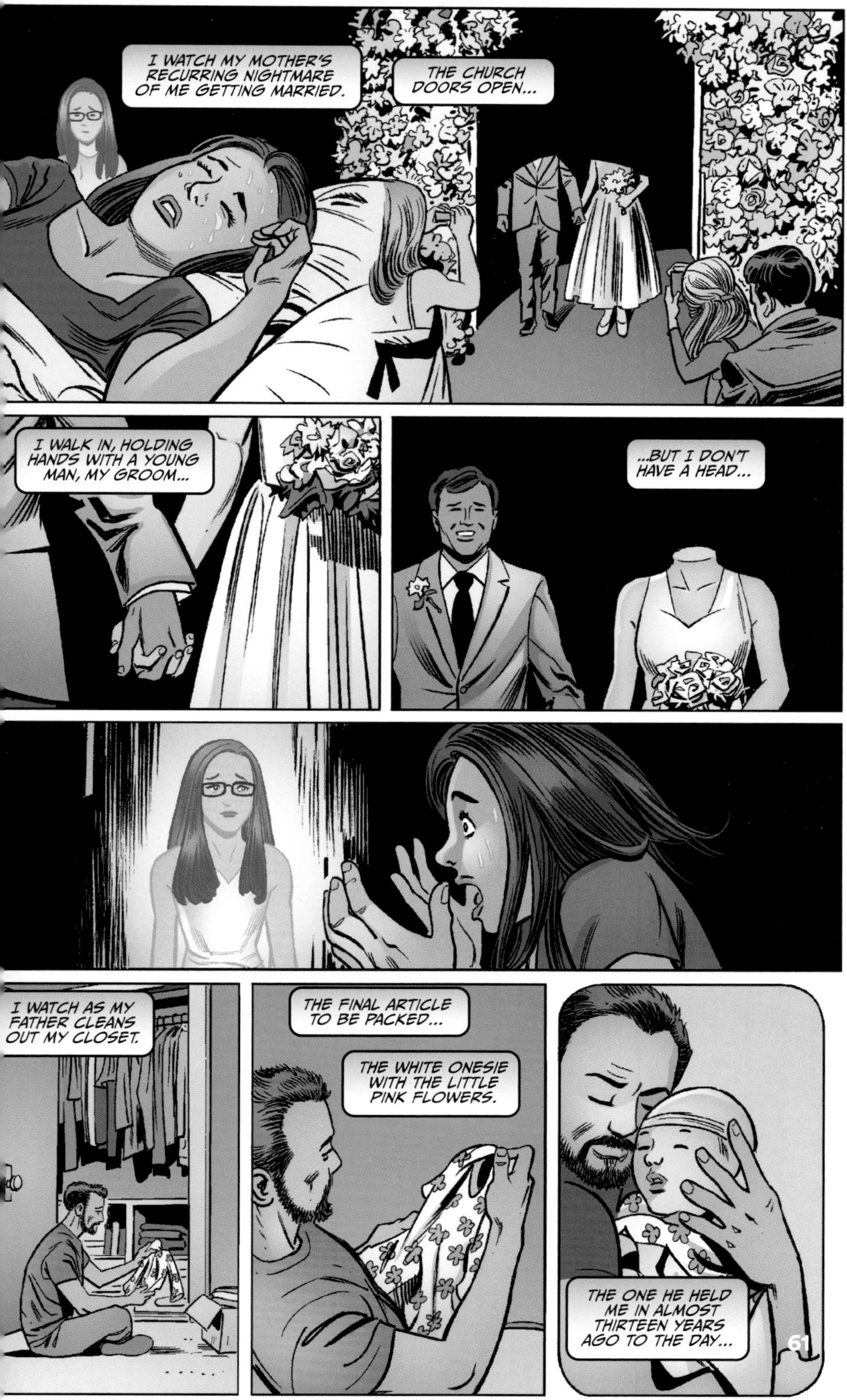
I WATCH MY MOTHER'S RECURRING NIGHTMARE OF ME GETTING MARRIED.
THE CHURCH DOORS OPEN...
I WALK IN, HOLDING HANDS WITH A YOUNG MAN, MY GROOM...
...BUT I DON'T HAVE A HEAD...
I WATCH AS MY FATHER CLEANS OUT MY CLOSET.
THE FINAL ARTICLE TO BE PACKED...
THE WHITE ONESIE WITH THE LITTLE PINK FLOWERS.
THE ONE HE HELD ME IN ALMOST THIRTEEN YEARS AGO TO THE DAY...

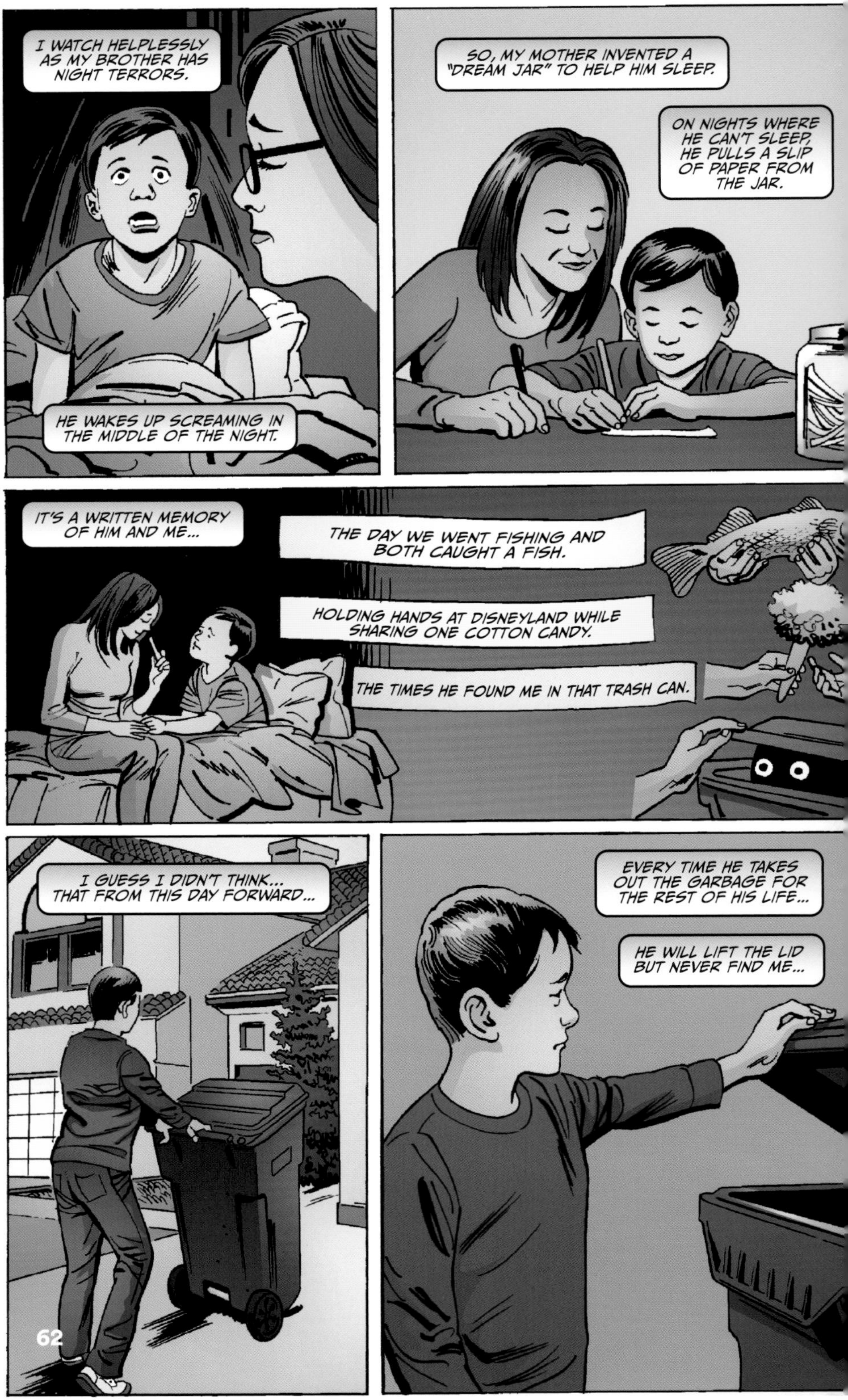
I WATCH HELPLESSLY AS MY BROTHER HAS NIGHT TERRORS.
HE WAKES UP SCREAMING IN THE MIDDLE OF THE NIGHT.
SO, MY MOTHER INVENTED A "DREAM JAR" TO HELP HIM SLEEP.
ON NIGHTS WHERE HE CAN'T SLEEP, HE PULLS A SLIP OF PAPER FROM THE JAR.
IT'S A WRITTEN MEMORY OF HIM AND ME...
THE DAY WE WENT FISHING AND BOTH CAUGHT A FISH.
HOLDING HANDS AT DISNEYLAND WHILE SHARING ONE COTTON CANDY.
THE TIMES HE FOUND ME IN THAT TRASH CAN.
I GUESS I DIDN'T THINK... THAT FROM THIS DAY FORWARD...
EVERY TIME HE TAKES OUT THE GARBAGE FOR THE REST OF HIS LIFE...
HE WILL LIFT THE LID BUT NEVER FIND ME...

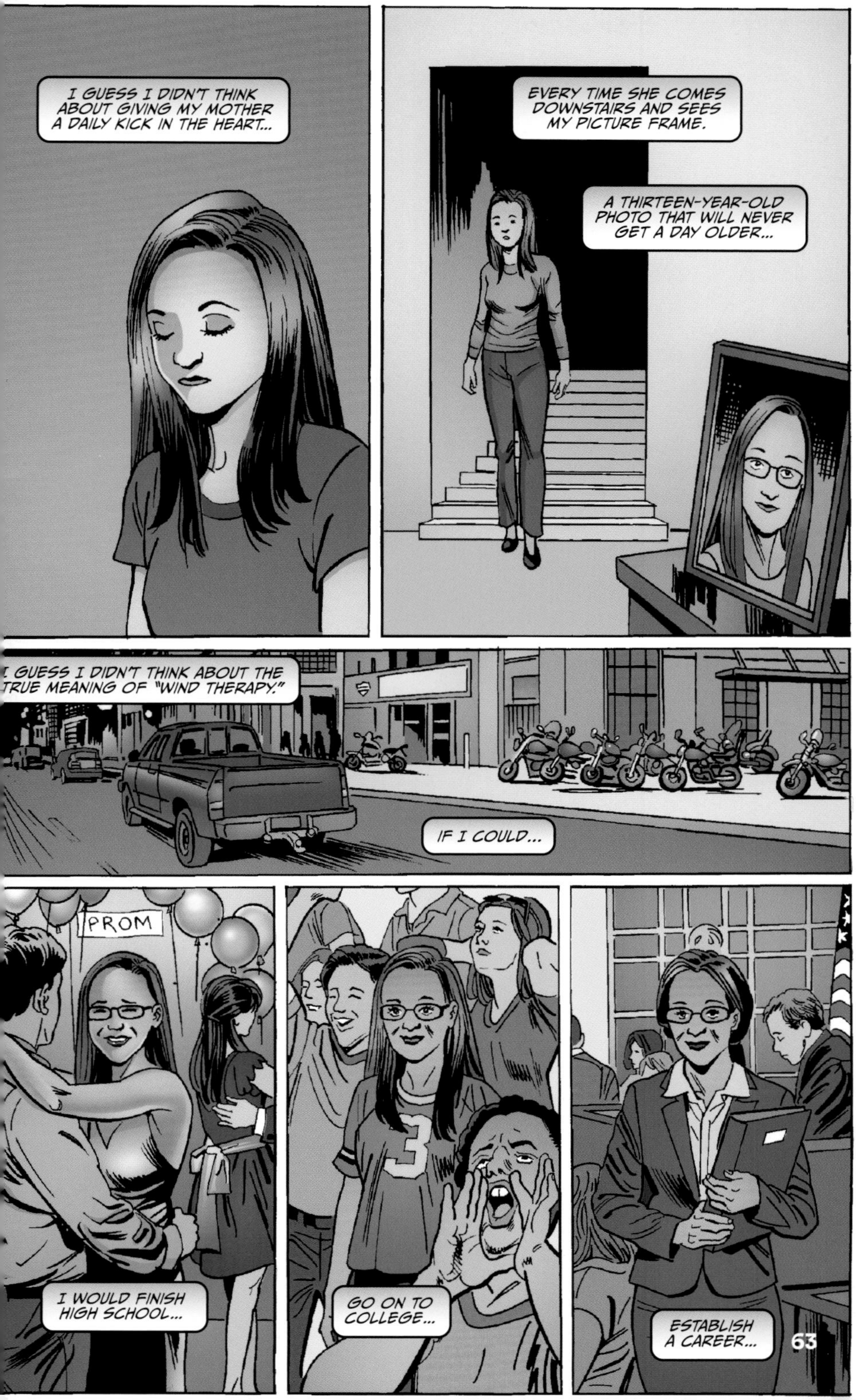
I GUESS I DIDN'T THINK ABOUT GIVING MY MOTHER A DAILY KICK IN THE HEART...
EVERY TIME SHE COMES DOWNSTAIRS AND SEES MY PICTURE FRAME.
A THIRTEEN-YEAR-OLD PHOTO THAT WILL NEVER GET A DAY OLDER...
I GUESS I DIDN'T THINK ABOUT THE TRUE MEANING OF "WIND THERAPY."
IF I COULD...
PROM
I WOULD FINISH HIGH SCHOOL...
3
GO ON TO COLLEGE...
ESTABLISH A CAREER...

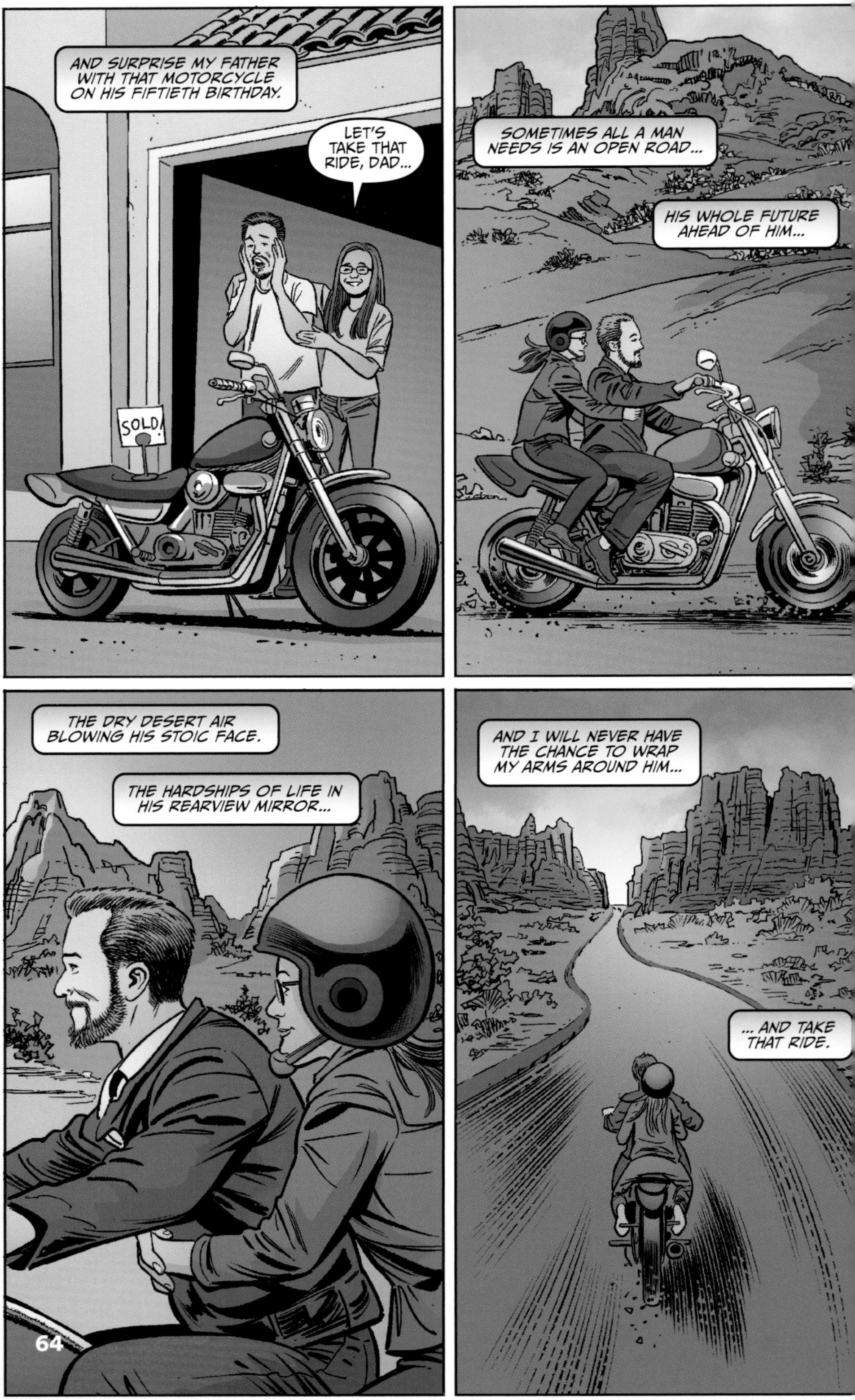
AND SURPRISE MY FATHER WITH THAT MOTORCYCLE ON HIS FIFTIETH BIRTHDAY.
LET'S TAKE THAT RIDE, DAD...
SOLD!
SOMETIMES ALL A MAN NEEDS IS AN OPEN ROAD...
HIS WHOLE FUTURE AHEAD OF HIM...
THE DRY DESERT AIR BLOWING HIS STOIC FACE.
THE HARDSHIPS OF LIFE IN HIS REARVIEW MIRROR...
AND I WILL NEVER HAVE THE CHANCE TO WRAP MY ARMS AROUND HIM...
... AND TAKE THAT RIDE.

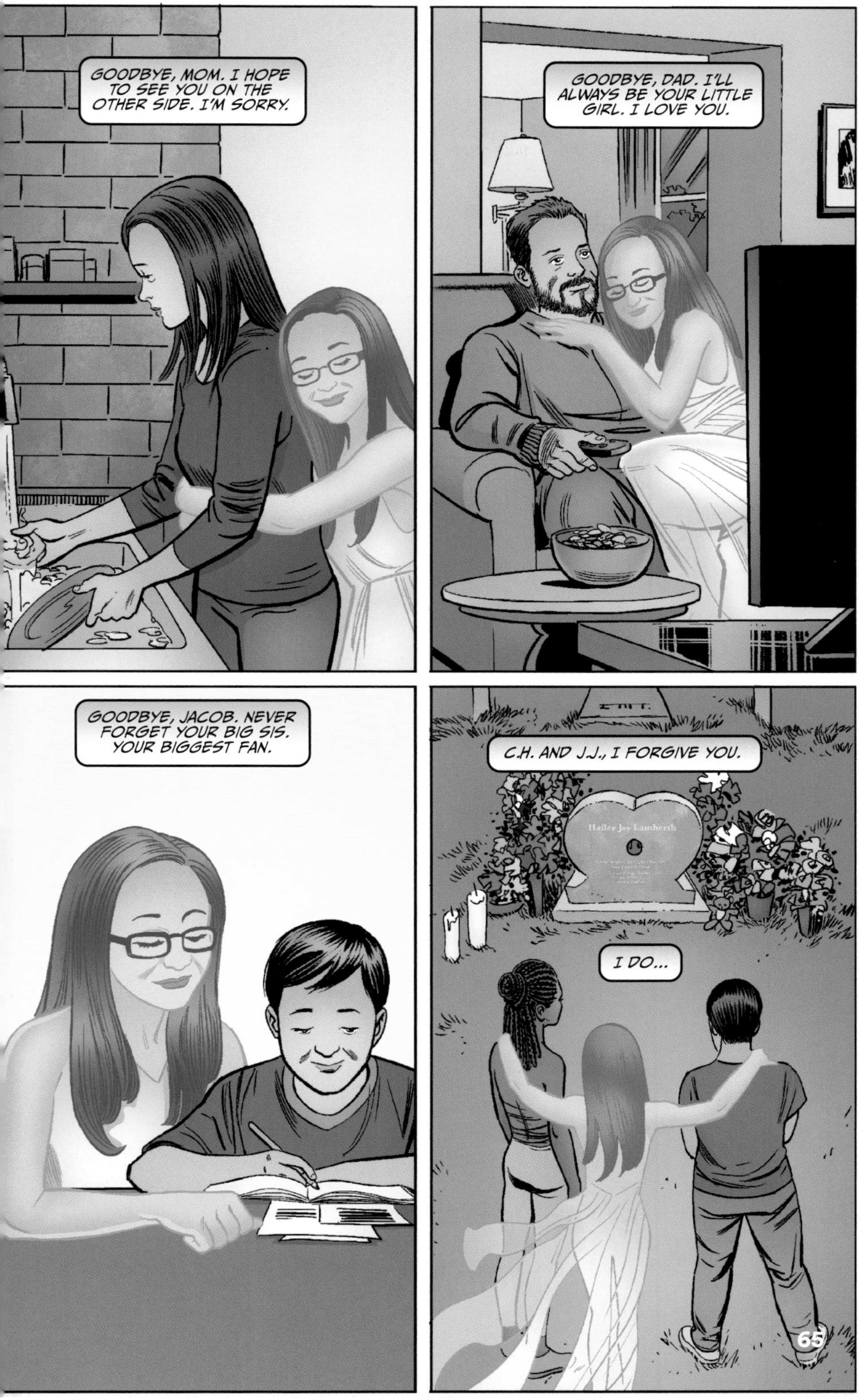
GOODBYE, MOM. I HOPE TO SEE YOU ON THE OTHER SIDE. I'M SORRY.
GOODBYE, DAD. I'LL ALWAYS BE YOUR LITTLE GIRL. I LOVE YOU.
GOODBYE, JACOB. NEVER FORGET YOUR BIG SIS. YOUR BIGGEST FAN.
C.H. AND J.J., I FORGIVE YOU.
Hailee Joy Lamberth
I DO...

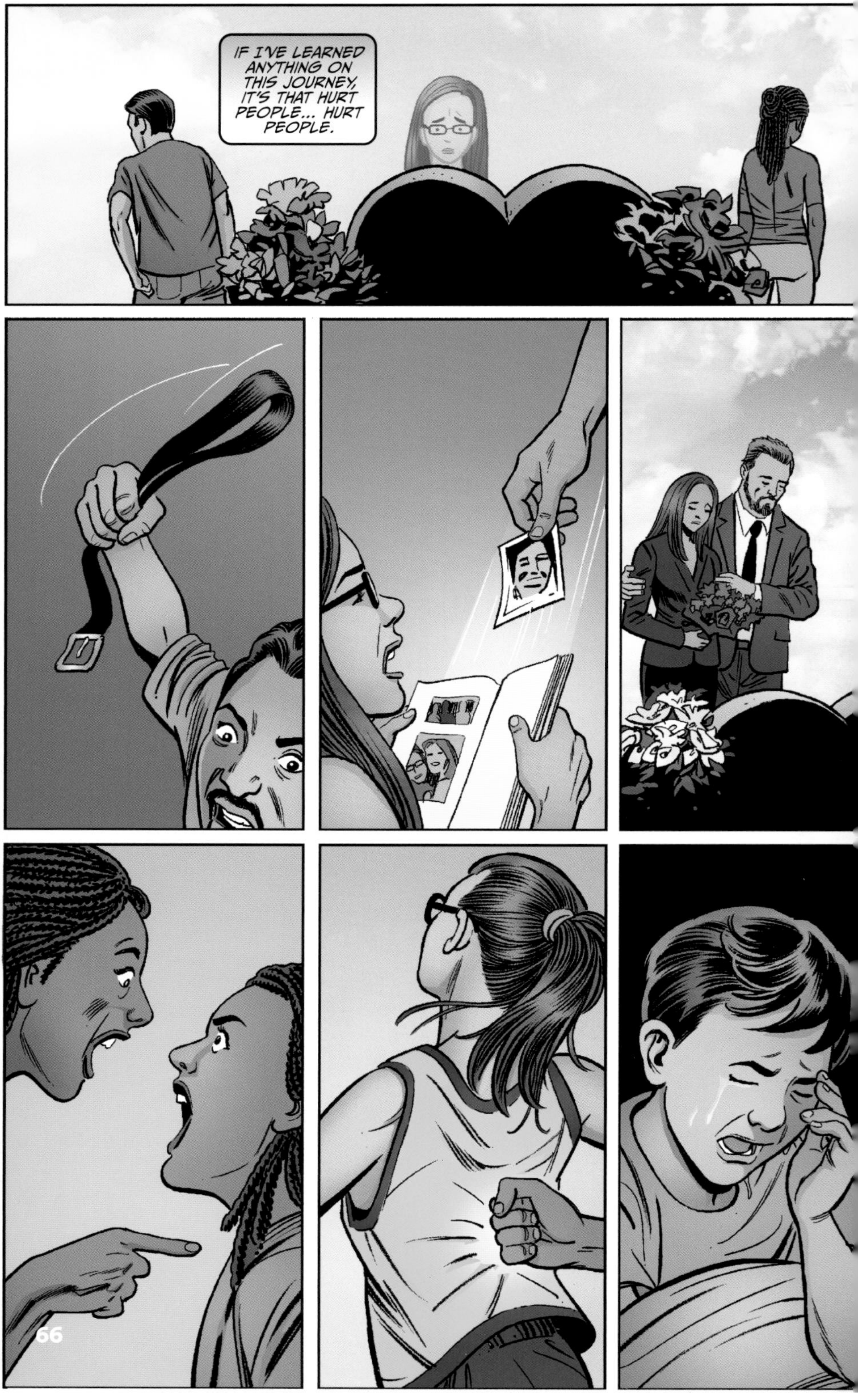
IF I'VE LEARNED ANYTHING ON THIS JOURNEY, IT'S THAT HURT PEOPLE... HURT PEOPLE.

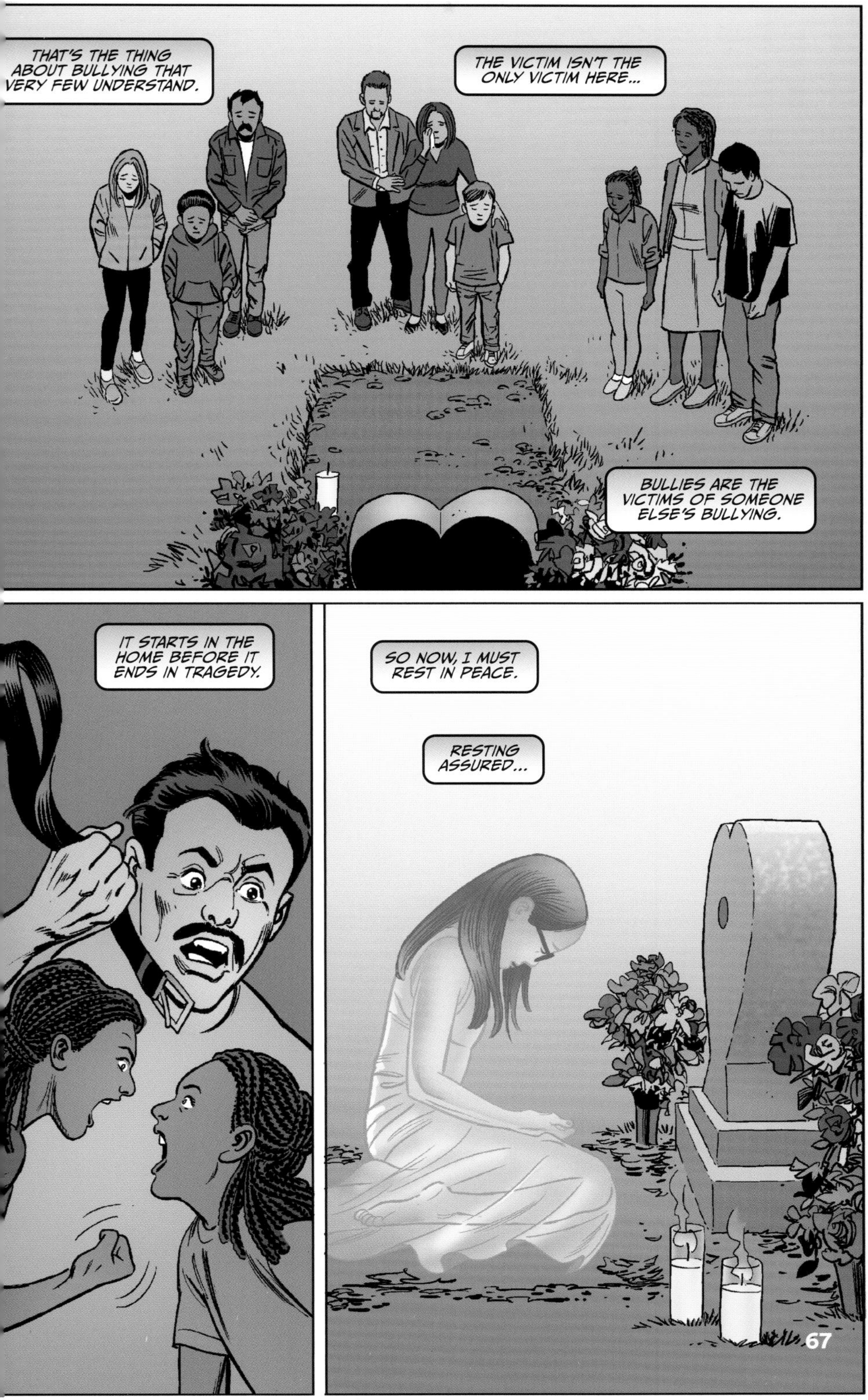
THAT'S THE THING ABOUT BULLYING THAT VERY FEW UNDERSTAND.
THE VICTIM ISN'T THE ONLY VICTIM HERE...
BULLIES ARE THE VICTIMS OF SOMEONE ELSE'S BULLYING.
IT STARTS IN THE HOME BEFORE IT ENDS IN TRAGEDY.
SO NOW, I MUST REST IN PEACE.
RESTING ASSURED...

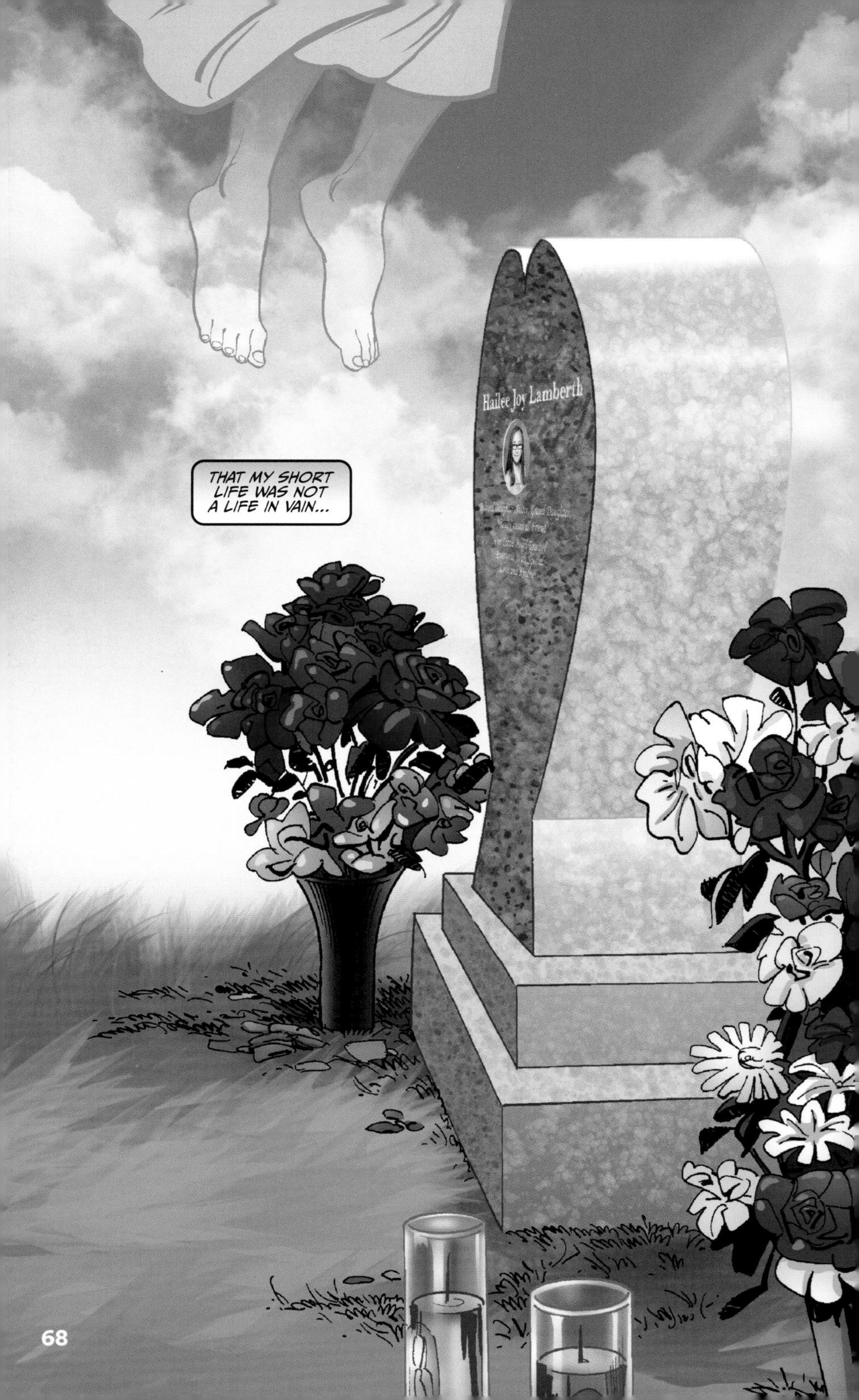
THAT MY SHORT LIFE WAS NOT A LIFE IN VAIN...
Hailee Joy Lamberth

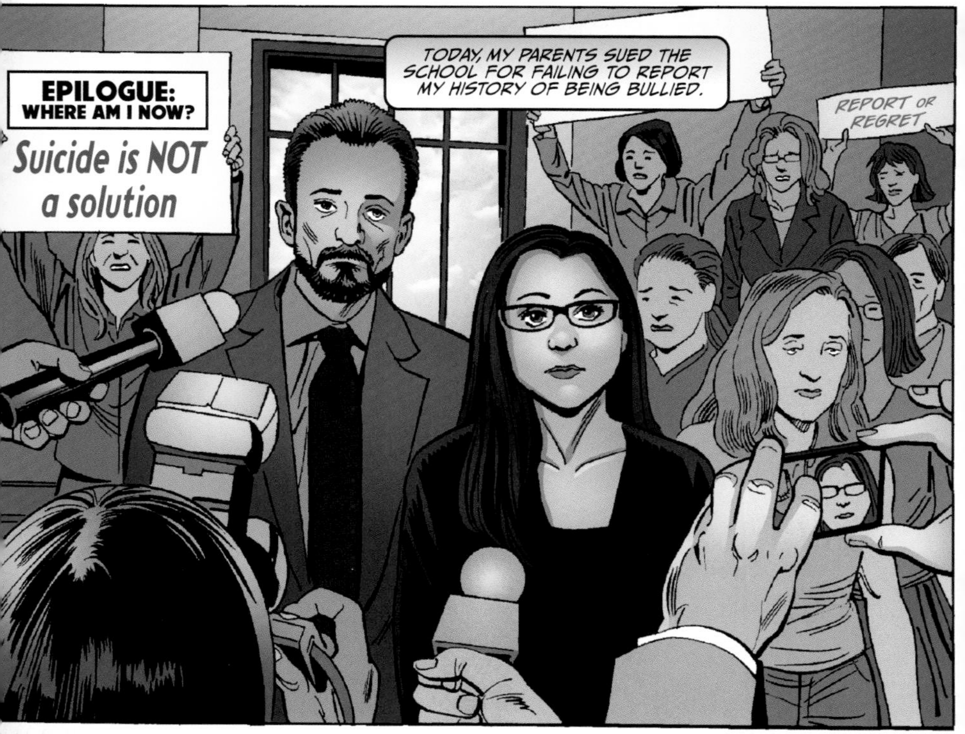
EPILOGUE:
WHERE AM I NOW?
Suicide is NOT a solution
TODAY, MY PARENTS SUED THE SCHOOL FOR FAILING TO REPORT MY HISTORY OF BEING BULLIED.
REPORT OR REGRET

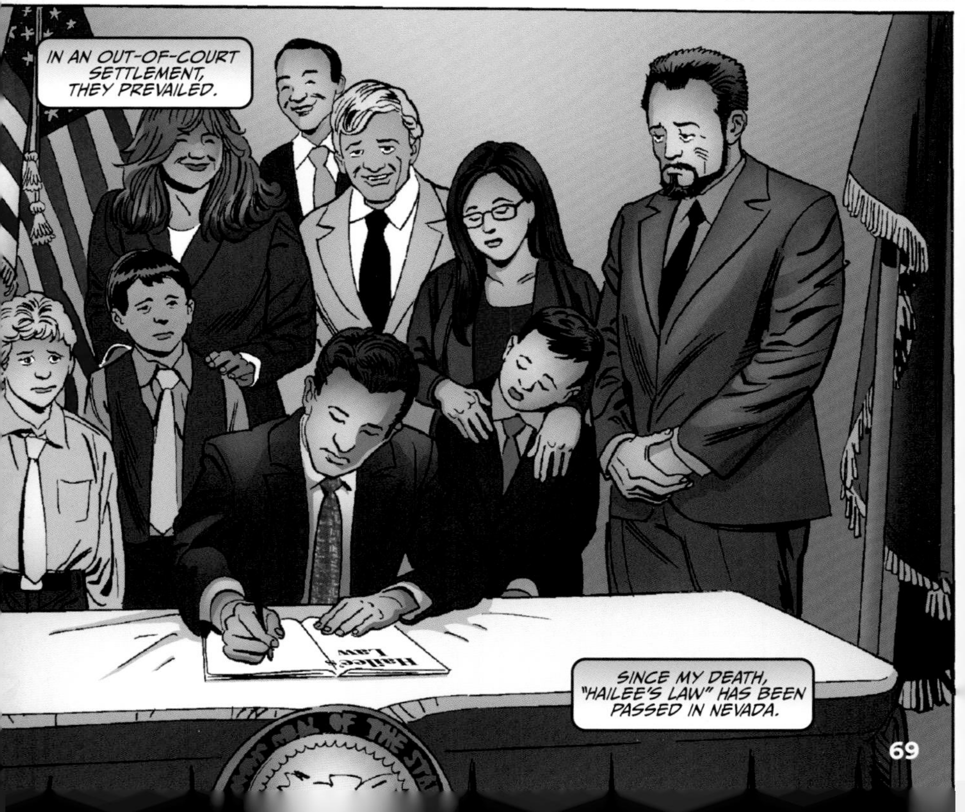
IN AN OUT-OF-COURT SETTLEMENT, THEY PREVAILED.
Hailee's Law
SINCE MY DEATH, "HAILEE'S LAW" HAS BEEN PASSED IN NEVADA.

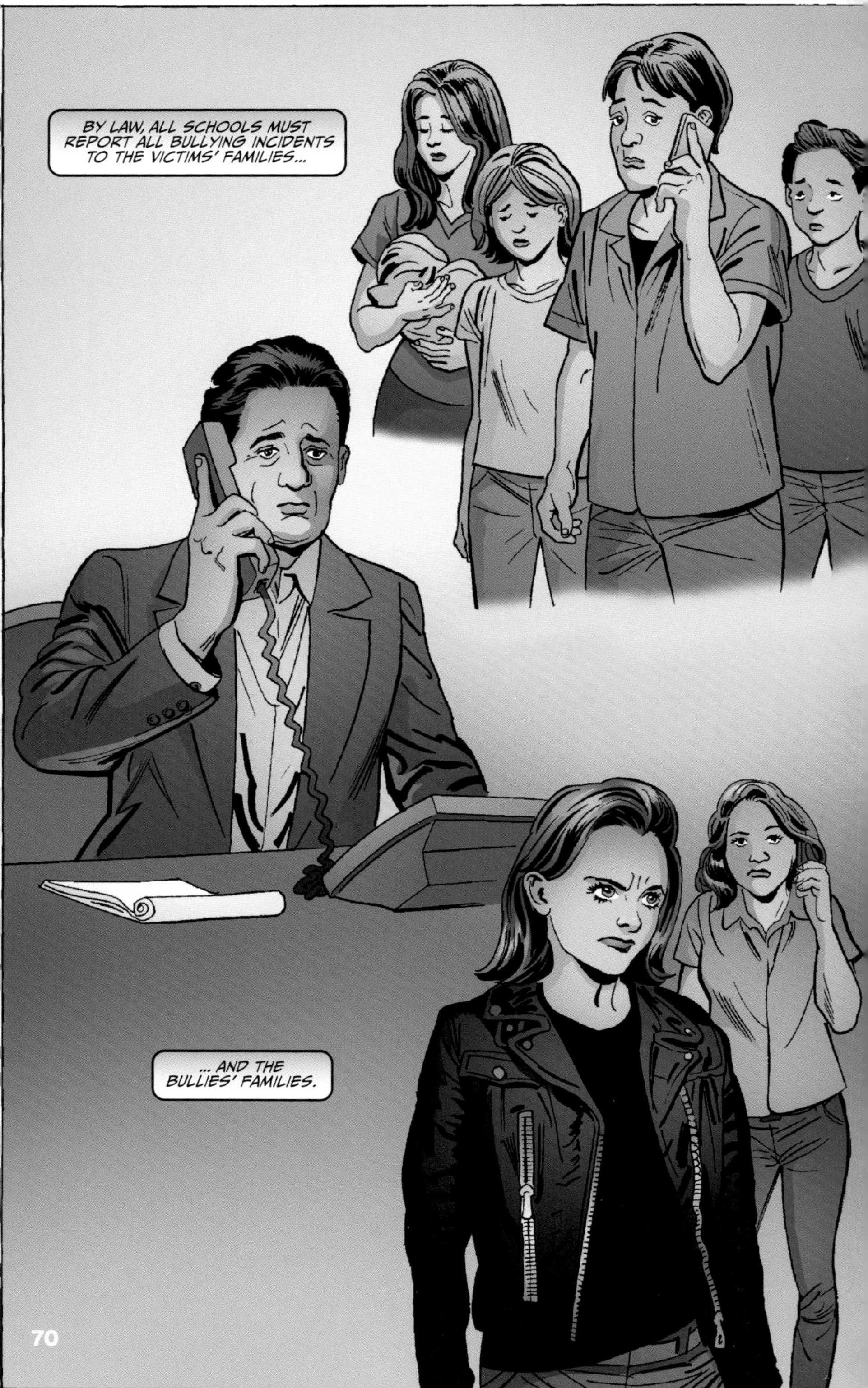
BY LAW, ALL SCHOOLS MUST REPORT ALL BULLYING INCIDENTS TO THE VICTIMS' FAMILIES...
... AND THE BULLIES' FAMILIES.

IF NOT, A TEACHER, OR A SCHOOL, COULD LOSE THEIR LICENSE AND EVEN BE PROSECUTED.

MY SCHOOL NEVER REPORTED IT. EVEN AFTER THE SUBSTITUTE TEACHER ALERTED THE PRINCIPAL.

IN MY SUICIDE NOTE, I ASKED THAT MY PARENTS TELL THE SCHOOL WHAT THOSE BULLIES DID TO ME.

TO THE KIDS OUT THERE, I HOPE THAT LOSING MY LIFE SAVES YOURS.

I want you to tell my school

IF I HAD IT TO DO OVER AGAIN, I WOULD'VE TOLD SOMEONE... CONSIDERED OPTIONS THAT HONESTLY, I NEVER KNEW I HAD.

CHANGED SCHOOLS.

WELCOME TO RENO

CHANGED CITIES.

CHANGED MINDSET.

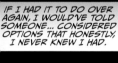

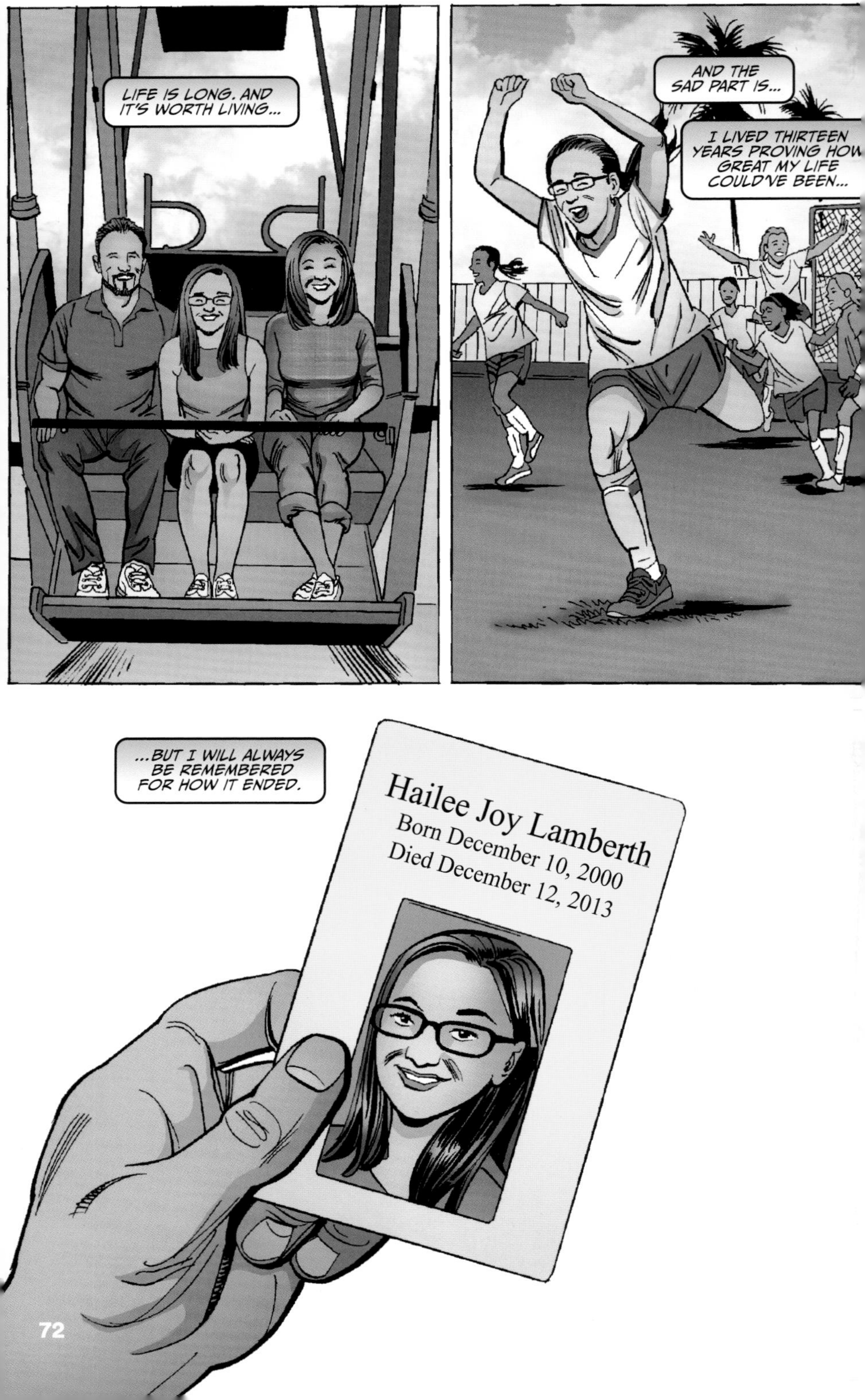
LIFE IS LONG. AND IT'S WORTH LIVING...
AND THE SAD PART IS...
I LIVED THIRTEEN YEARS PROVING HOW GREAT MY LIFE COULD'VE BEEN...
...BUT I WILL ALWAYS BE REMEMBERED FOR HOW IT ENDED.
Hailee Joy Lamberth
Born December 10, 2000
Died December 12, 2013

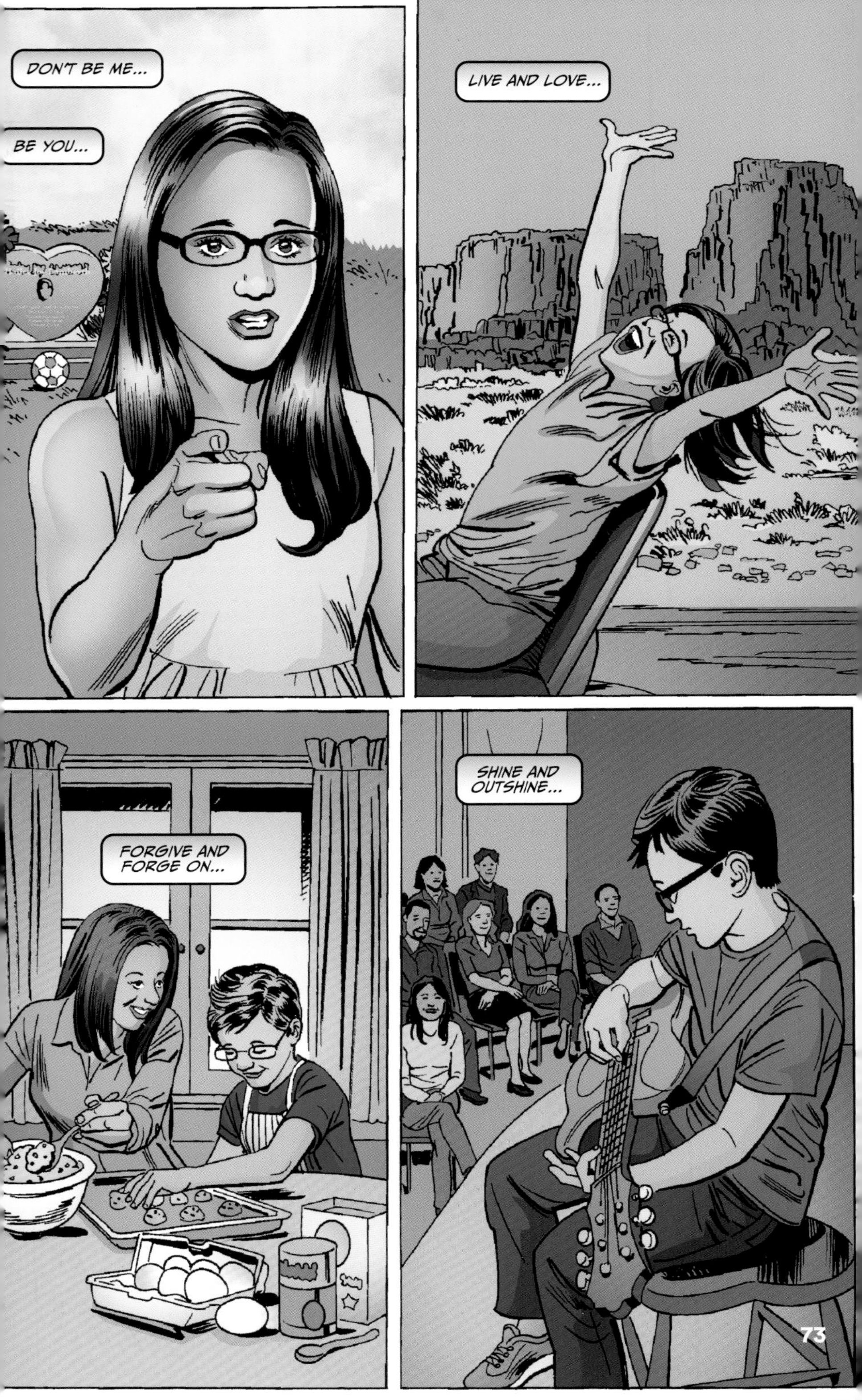
DON'T BE ME...
BE YOU...
LIVE AND LOVE...
FORGIVE AND FORGE ON...
SHINE AND OUTSHINE...

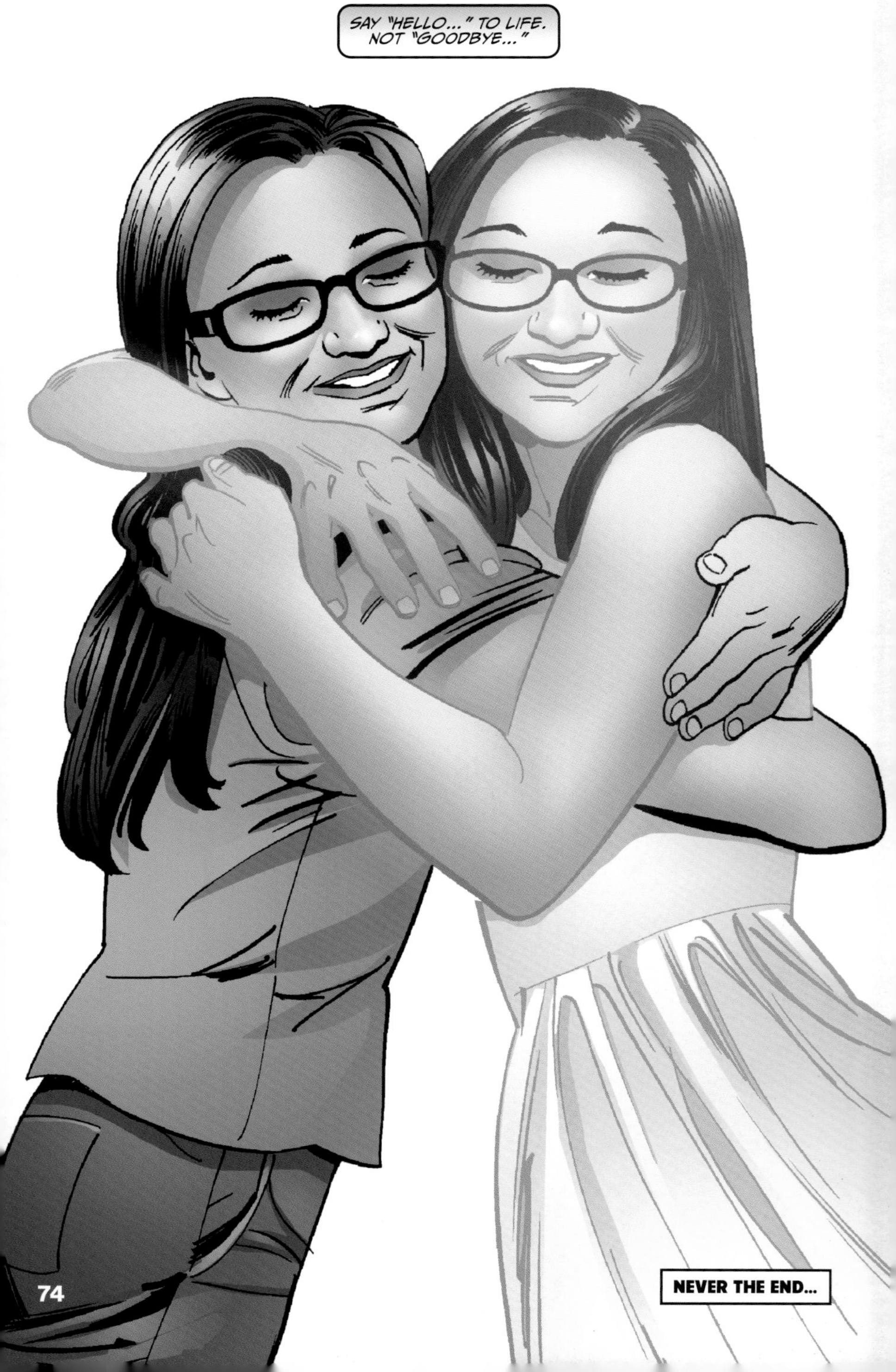
SAY "HELLO..." TO LIFE. NOT "GOODBYE..."
NEVER THE END...

ABOUT THE AUTHOR

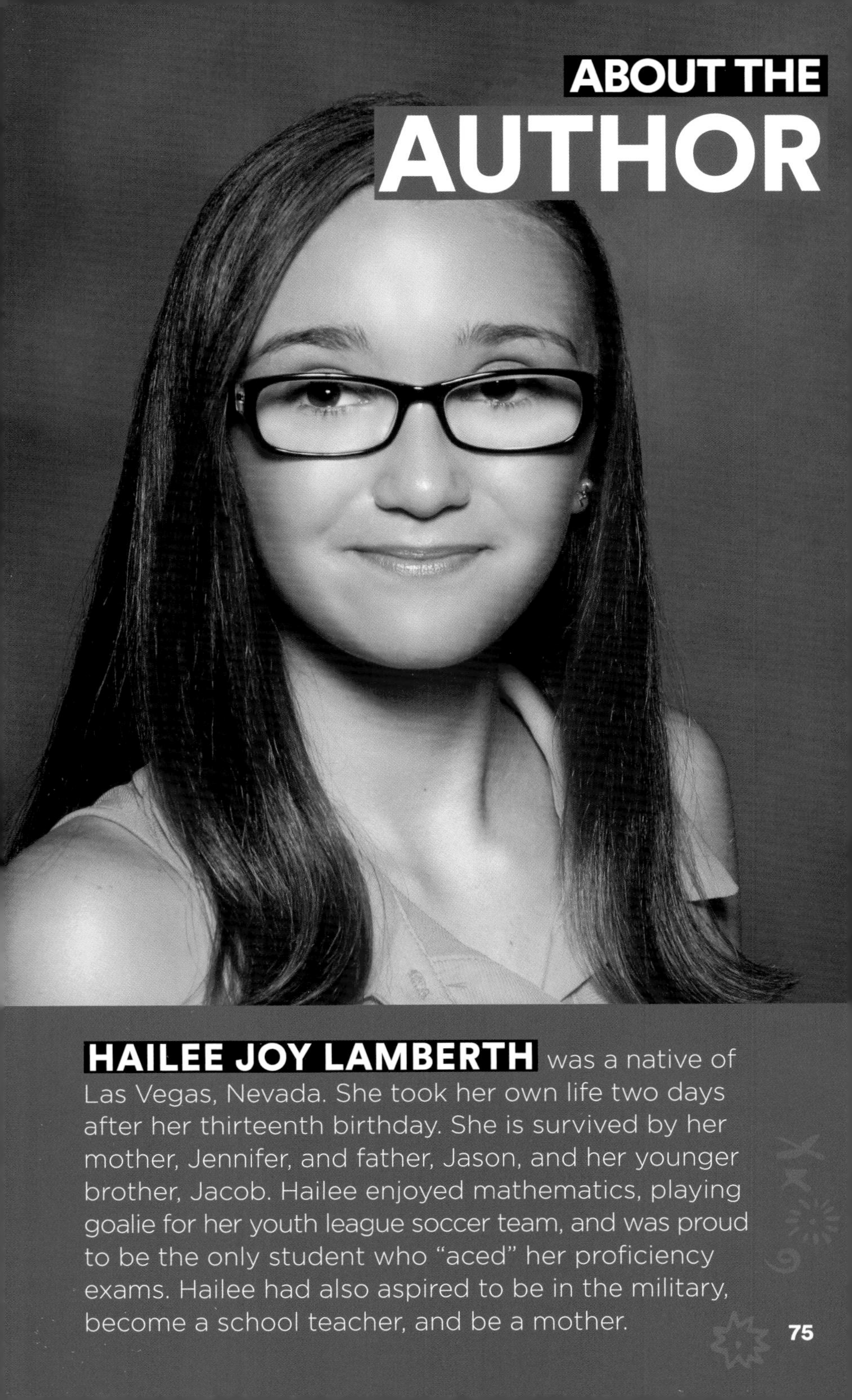

HAILEE JOY LAMBERTH was a native of Las Vegas, Nevada. She took her own life two days after her thirteenth birthday. She is survived by her mother, Jennifer, and father, Jason, and her younger brother, Jacob. Hailee enjoyed mathematics, playing goalie for her youth league soccer team, and was proud to be the only student who "aced" her proficiency exams. Hailee had also aspired to be in the military, become a school teacher, and be a mother.

HAILEE...

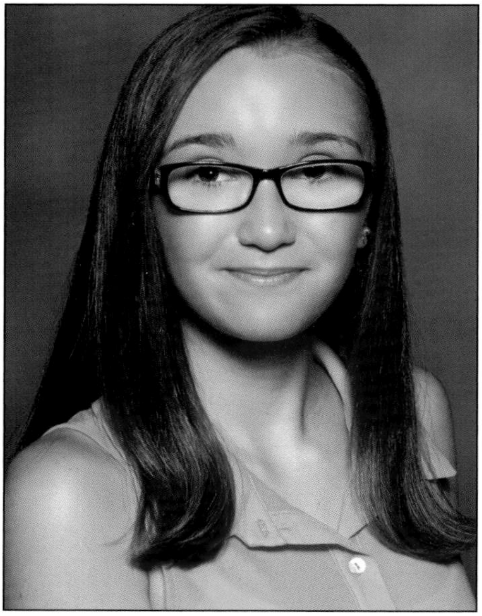

Hailee's seventh grade school photo.

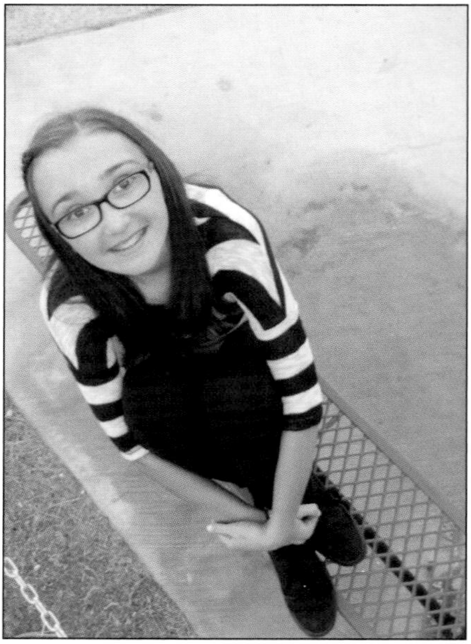

Seventh grade newspaper photo.

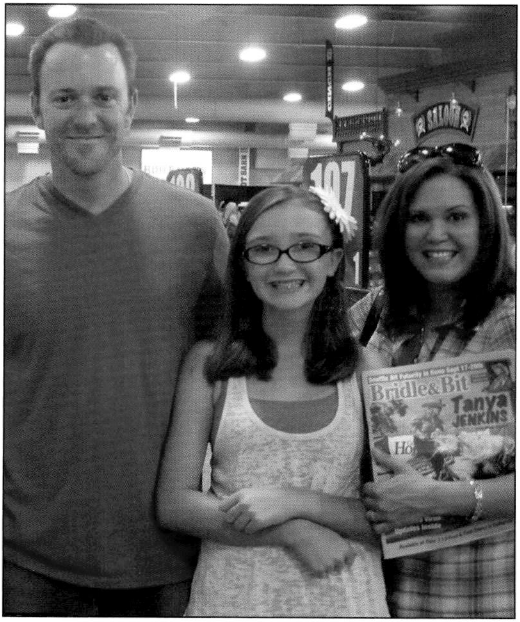
SALOON
107
Bridle&Bit
Tanya
JENKINS

South Point Casino Horse Show, October 2012.

...HAILEE

Soccer tournament.

Thanksgiving, 2011.

Hiking at Mt. Charleston.

Camping at Lake Mead.

HAILEE...

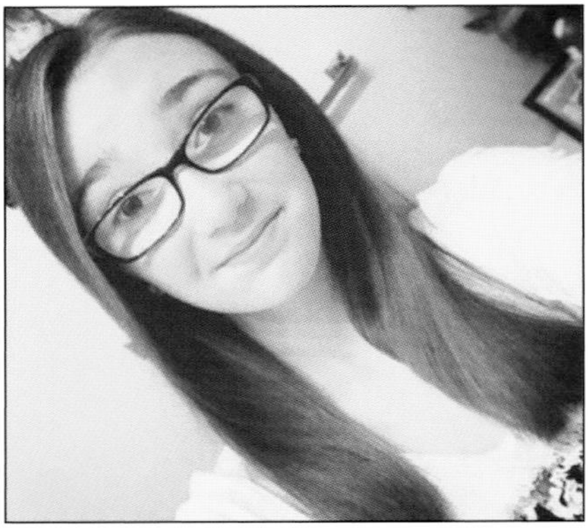
Hailee's selfie on her thirteenth birthday.

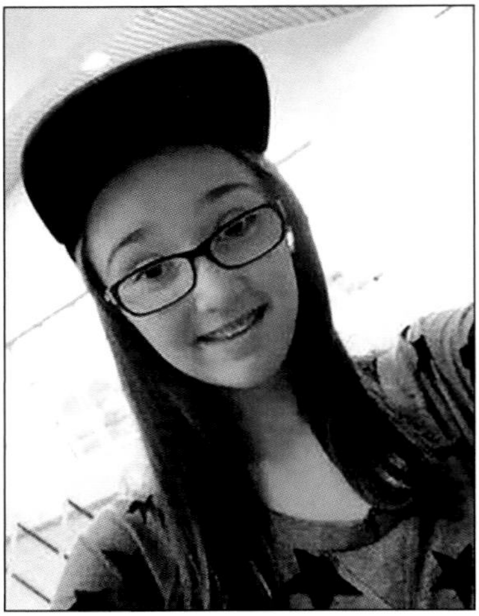
Selfie, 2012.

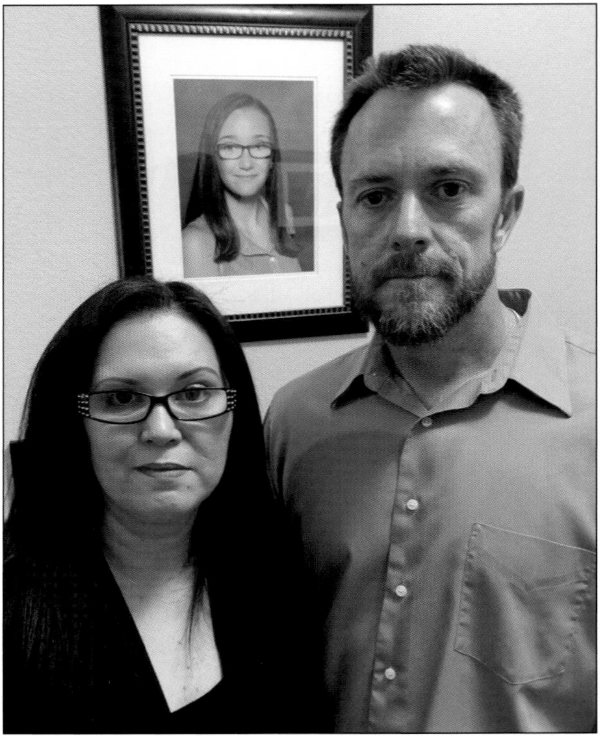
Hailee's mom and dad.

TAKE 5!

FIVE PARENT TAKE-AWAYS ABOUT SUICIDE

LORRAN GARRISON

Lorran Garrison is a school psychologist in San Diego, and has spoken about mental health awareness and suicide ideation at Comic-Con International: San Diego and other conventions. She is also the co-founder of Little Brain Storm, which recently released *Brain Boy and Bob: The Very Hungry Maggot*. This is the first in a series that explores and educates about disabilities and other issues with the goal of ending the stigma of mental illness.

IF YOUR CHILD APPEARS SELF-DESTRUCTIVE, TAKE IT SERIOUSLY.

Do not keep it a secret, get help. People who are suicidal usually give warning signs, often to a parent, friend, teacher, or anyone else in their lives. Take these signs seriously and never keep them a secret.

GET HELP!

Call 911 for emergency assistance if your child is at immediate risk. Other numbers to call are the **National Suicide Prevention Lifeline at 1-800-273-TALK or the Crisis Text Line (text "HOME" to 741741)**. Also get help from the school and/or community mental health resources as soon as possible.

WARNING SIGNS INCLUDE:

direct threats (*I'm going to kill myself*); indirect threats (*I want to sleep forever, wait until I'm gone, I have nothing to live for*); suicide notes and plans (on paper or online postings); prior suicidal behavior; making "final" arrangements (i.e., giving away prized possessions, making a will or funeral arrangements); self-harm; and preoccupation with death. There also may be changes in behavior, appearance, and expressed thoughts or feelings.

ASK YOUR CHILD, "ARE YOU THINKING OF SUICIDE?"

If your child confides in you, their peer, another trusted adult or even posts on social media that they are contemplating suicide, remain calm, listen to what they have to say, and focus your concern on their well-being. Do not blame or judge, reassure that this feeling is temporary and that there is help. Provide constant supervision and remove things that might cause self-harm. Suicide is preventable but it's the second leading cause of death for people in the United States between the ages of 15 and 24. We can all help stop suicidal thoughts from becoming action.

AFTER THE IMMEDIATE CRISIS IS OVER, KEEP COMMUNICATION OPEN.

Offer hope, don't judge. Help them by talking about what makes them feel grounded and connected with community, family, peers, religious and/or cultural beliefs that promote healthy living. Treatment may include talk therapy or medication. Let them know that these negative feelings are temporary. Remind them that they are loved, special, and important to you.

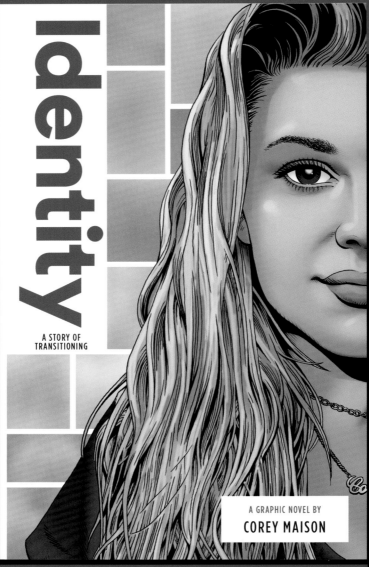

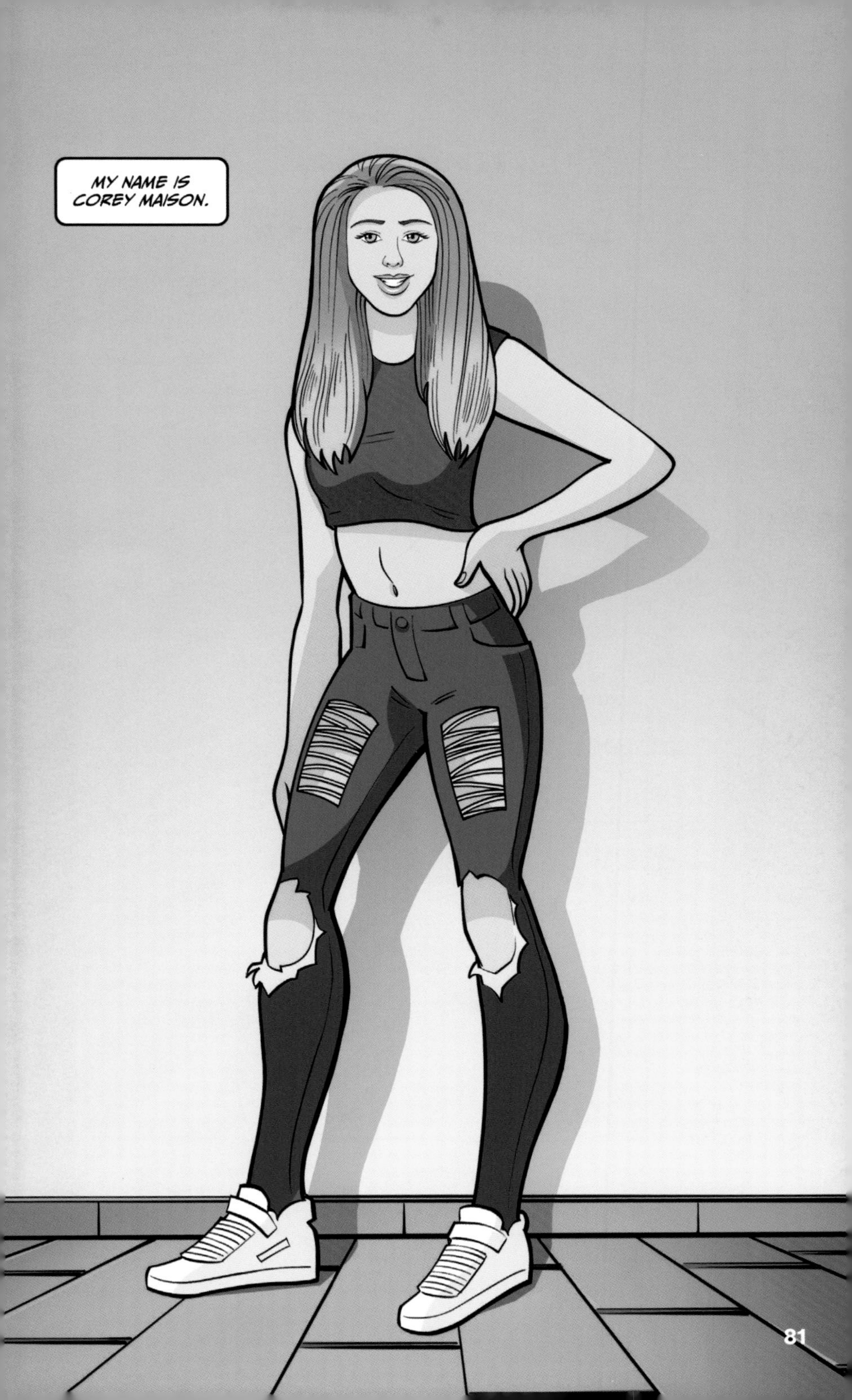
MY NAME IS
COREY MAISON.

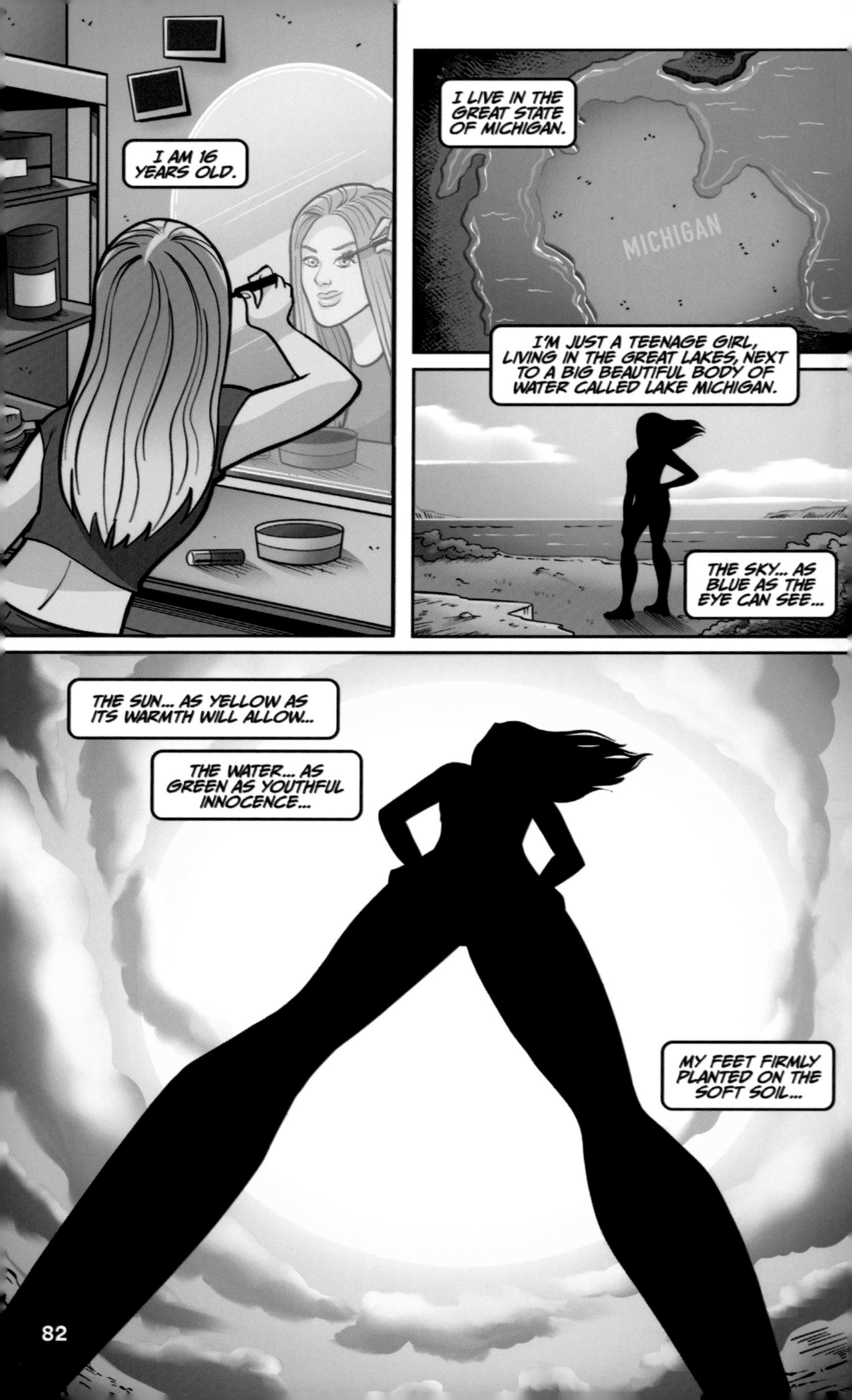
I AM 16 YEARS OLD.
I LIVE IN THE GREAT STATE OF MICHIGAN.
MICHIGAN
I'M JUST A TEENAGE GIRL, LIVING IN THE GREAT LAKES, NEXT TO A BIG BEAUTIFUL BODY OF WATER CALLED LAKE MICHIGAN.
THE SKY... AS BLUE AS THE EYE CAN SEE...
THE SUN... AS YELLOW AS ITS WARMTH WILL ALLOW...
THE WATER... AS GREEN AS YOUTHFUL INNOCENCE...
MY FEET FIRMLY PLANTED ON THE SOFT SOIL...

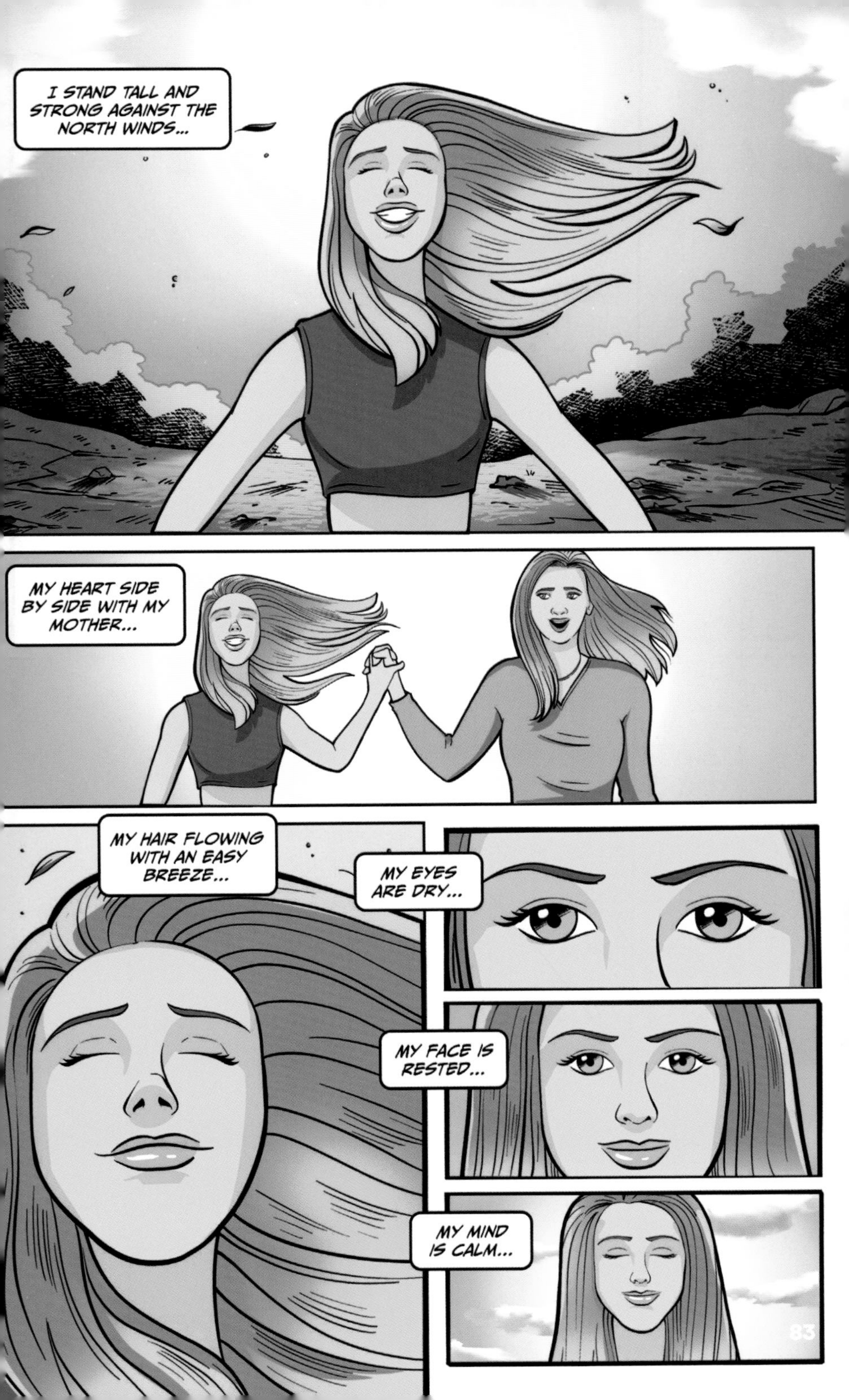
I STAND TALL AND STRONG AGAINST THE NORTH WINDS...
MY HEART SIDE BY SIDE WITH MY MOTHER...
MY HAIR FLOWING WITH AN EASY BREEZE...
MY EYES ARE DRY...
MY FACE IS RESTED...
MY MIND IS CALM...

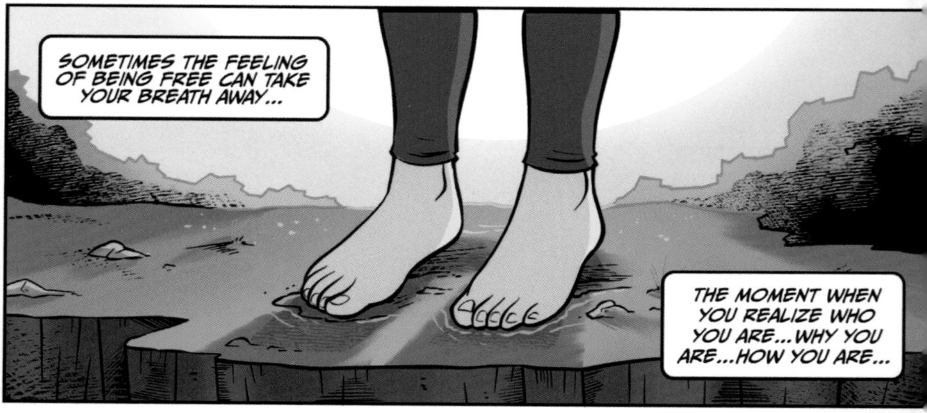
SOMETIMES THE FEELING OF BEING FREE CAN TAKE YOUR BREATH AWAY...
THE MOMENT WHEN YOU REALIZE WHO YOU ARE...WHY YOU ARE...HOW YOU ARE...

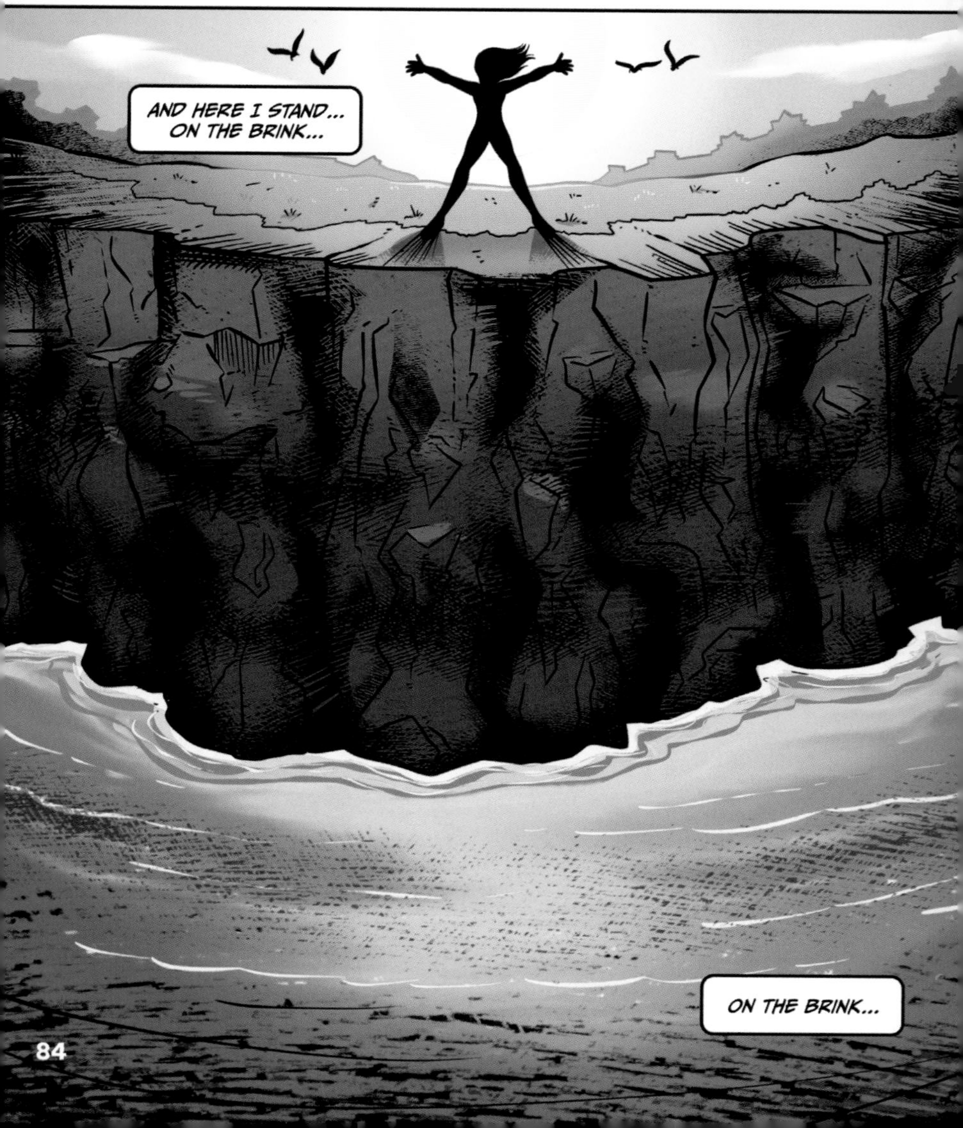
AND HERE I STAND... ON THE BRINK...
ON THE BRINK...

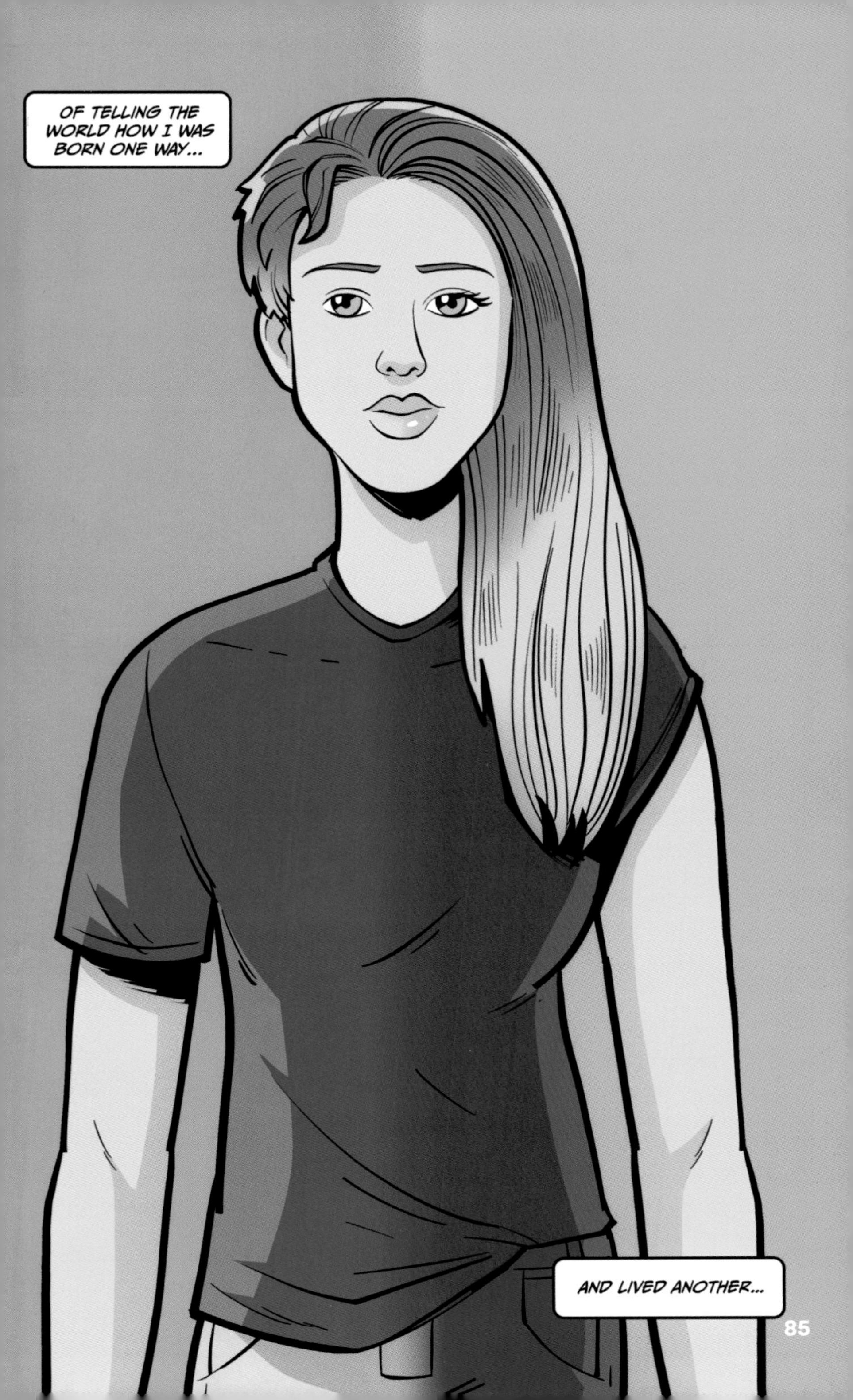
OF TELLING THE WORLD HOW I WAS BORN ONE WAY...
AND LIVED ANOTHER...

THIS...

...IS MY STORY.

I WAS BORN IN LAS VEGAS, NEVADA ON AUGUST 31, 2001.

I WAS A PERFECTLY NORMAL BABY. SIX POUNDS, THREE OUNCES.

...A PRETTY FACE WITH PRETTY PINK LIPS...

...TWO ARMS... TWO LEGS...

I HAD ALL OF MY FINGERS AND TOES...

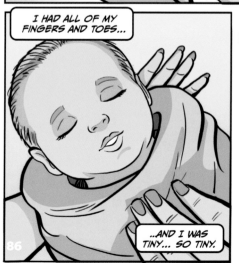

...AND I WAS TINY... SO TINY.

CONGRATULATIONS, IT'S A HEALTHY BABY BOY!

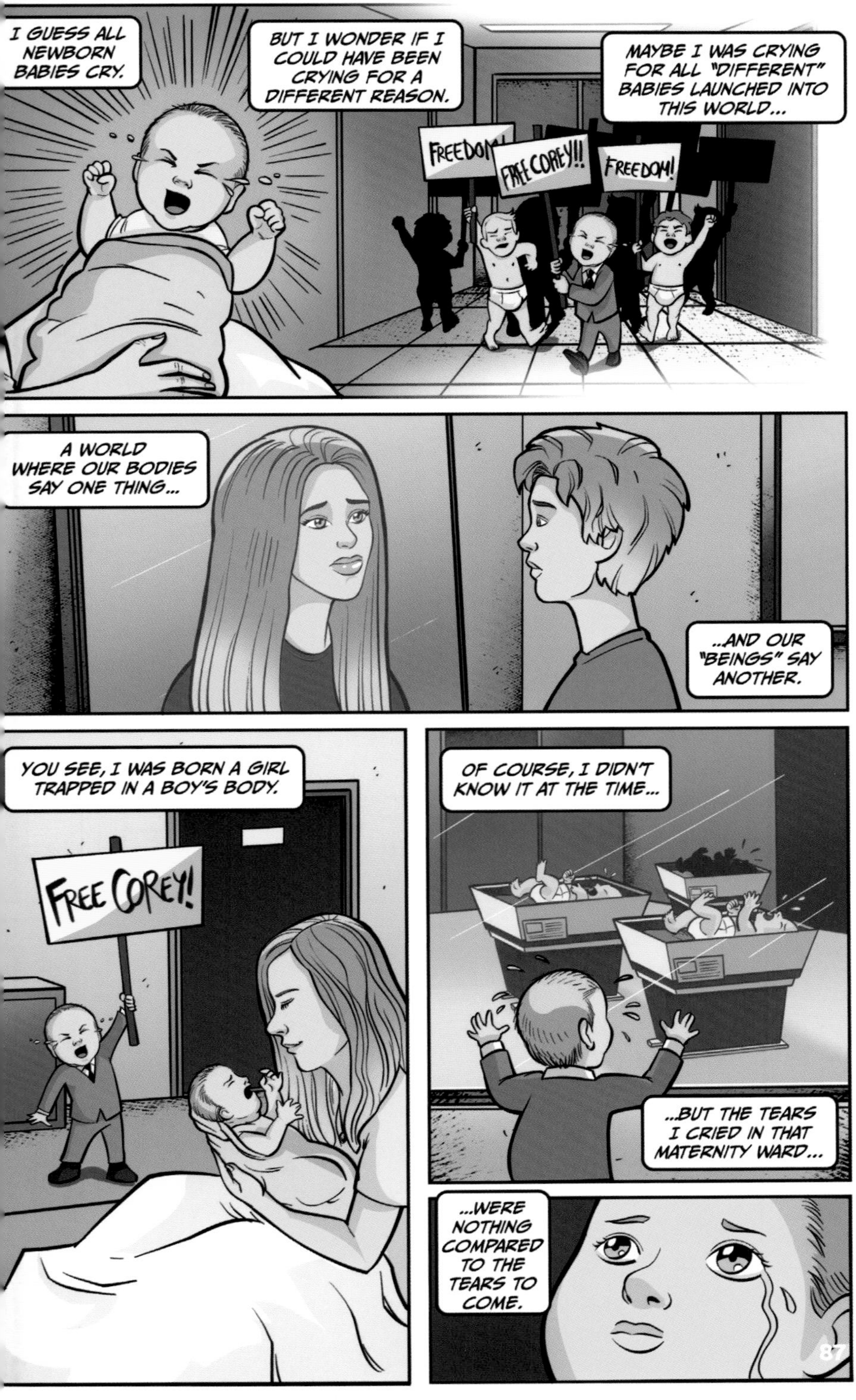

I GUESS ALL NEWBORN BABIES CRY.
BUT I WONDER IF I COULD HAVE BEEN CRYING FOR A DIFFERENT REASON.
MAYBE I WAS CRYING FOR ALL "DIFFERENT" BABIES LAUNCHED INTO THIS WORLD...
FREEDOM!
FREE COREY!!
FREEDOM!
A WORLD WHERE OUR BODIES SAY ONE THING...
...AND OUR "BEINGS" SAY ANOTHER.
YOU SEE, I WAS BORN A GIRL TRAPPED IN A BOY'S BODY.
FREE COREY!
OF COURSE, I DIDN'T KNOW IT AT THE TIME...
...BUT THE TEARS I CRIED IN THAT MATERNITY WARD...
...WERE NOTHING COMPARED TO THE TEARS TO COME.

AVAILABLE NOW...

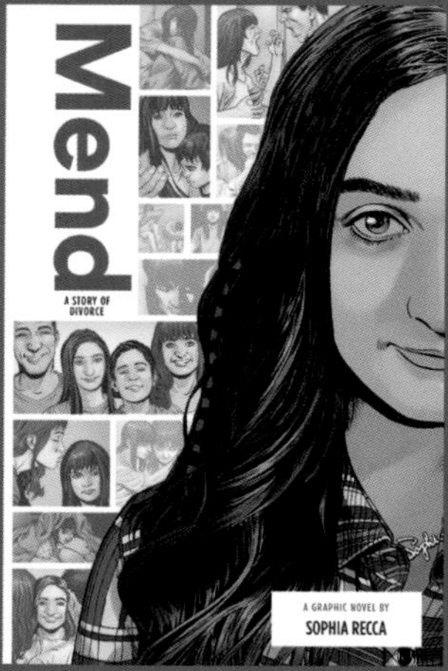
Mend
A STORY OF DIVORCE
A GRAPHIC NOVEL BY
SOPHIA RECCA

MEND: A STORY OF DIVORCE

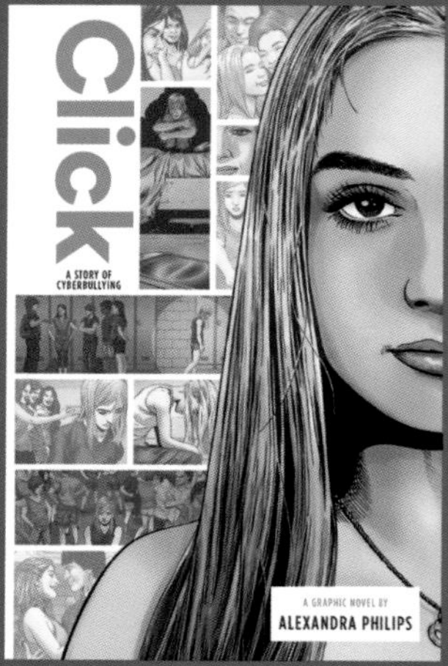
Click
A STORY OF CYBERBULLYING
A GRAPHIC NOVEL BY
ALEXANDRA PHILIPS

CLICK: A STORY OF CYBERBULLYING

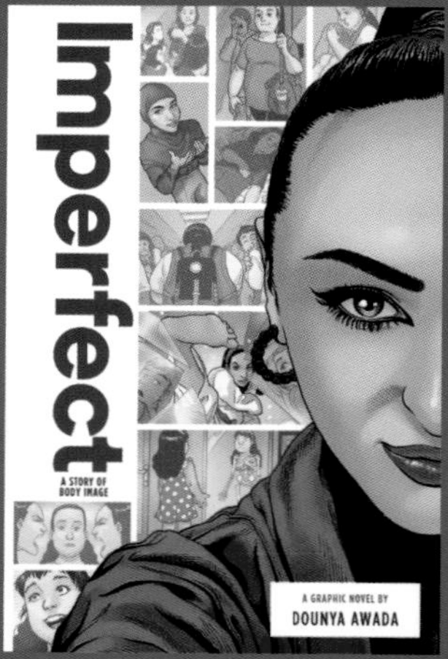
Imperfect
A STORY OF BODY IMAGE
A GRAPHIC NOVEL BY
DOUNYA AWADA

IMPERFECT: A STORY OF BODY IMAGE

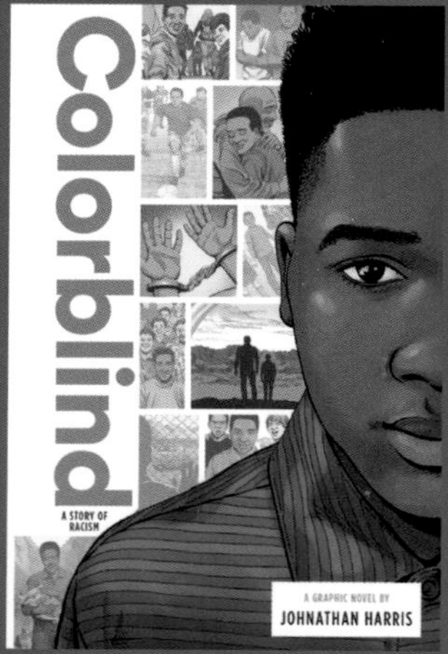
Colorblind
A STORY OF RACISM
A GRAPHIC NOVEL BY
JOHNATHAN HARRIS

COLORBLIND: A STORY OF RACISM

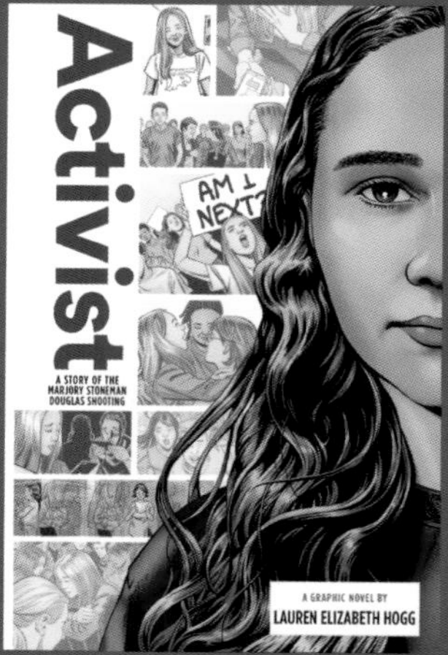
Activist
A STORY OF THE MARJORY STONEMAN DOUGLAS SHOOTING
AM I NEXT?
A GRAPHIC NOVEL BY
LAUREN ELIZABETH HOGG

ACTIVIST: A STORY OF THE MARJORY STONEMAN DOUGLAS SHOOTING

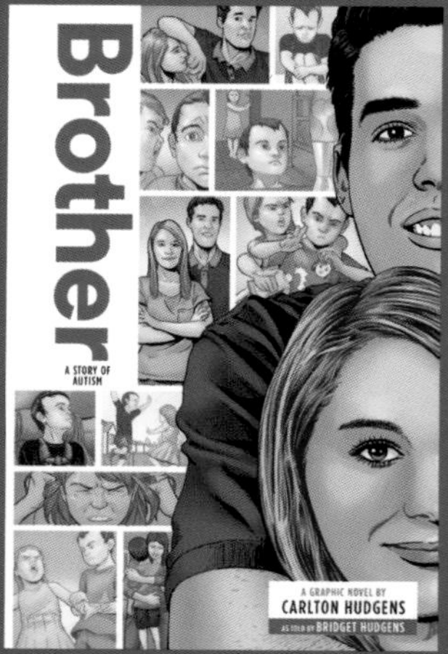
Brother
A STORY OF AUTISM
A GRAPHIC NOVEL BY
CARLTON HUDGENS
AS TOLD BY BRIDGET HUDGENS

BROTHER: A STORY OF AUTISM